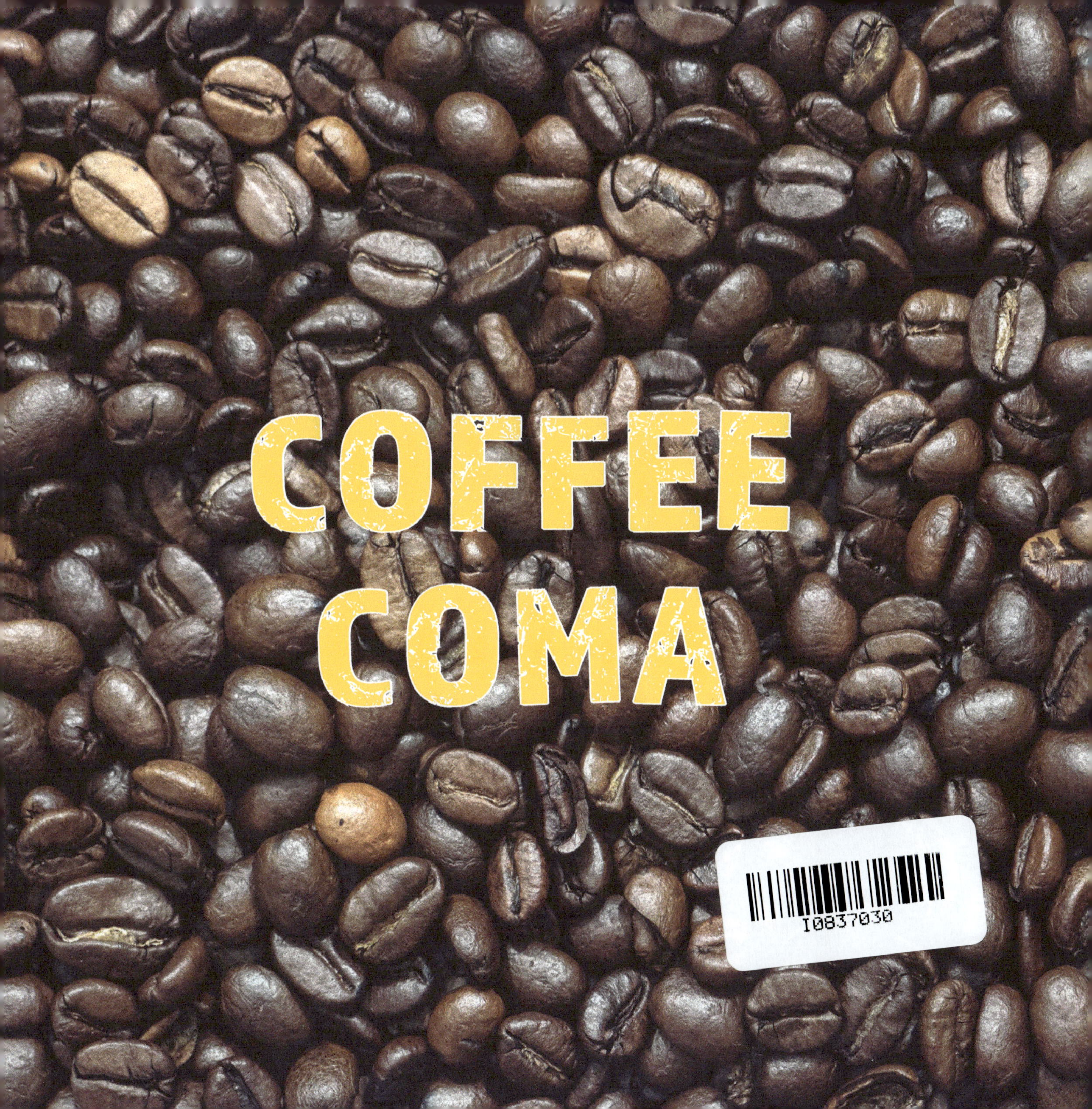
COFFEE
COMA
I0837030

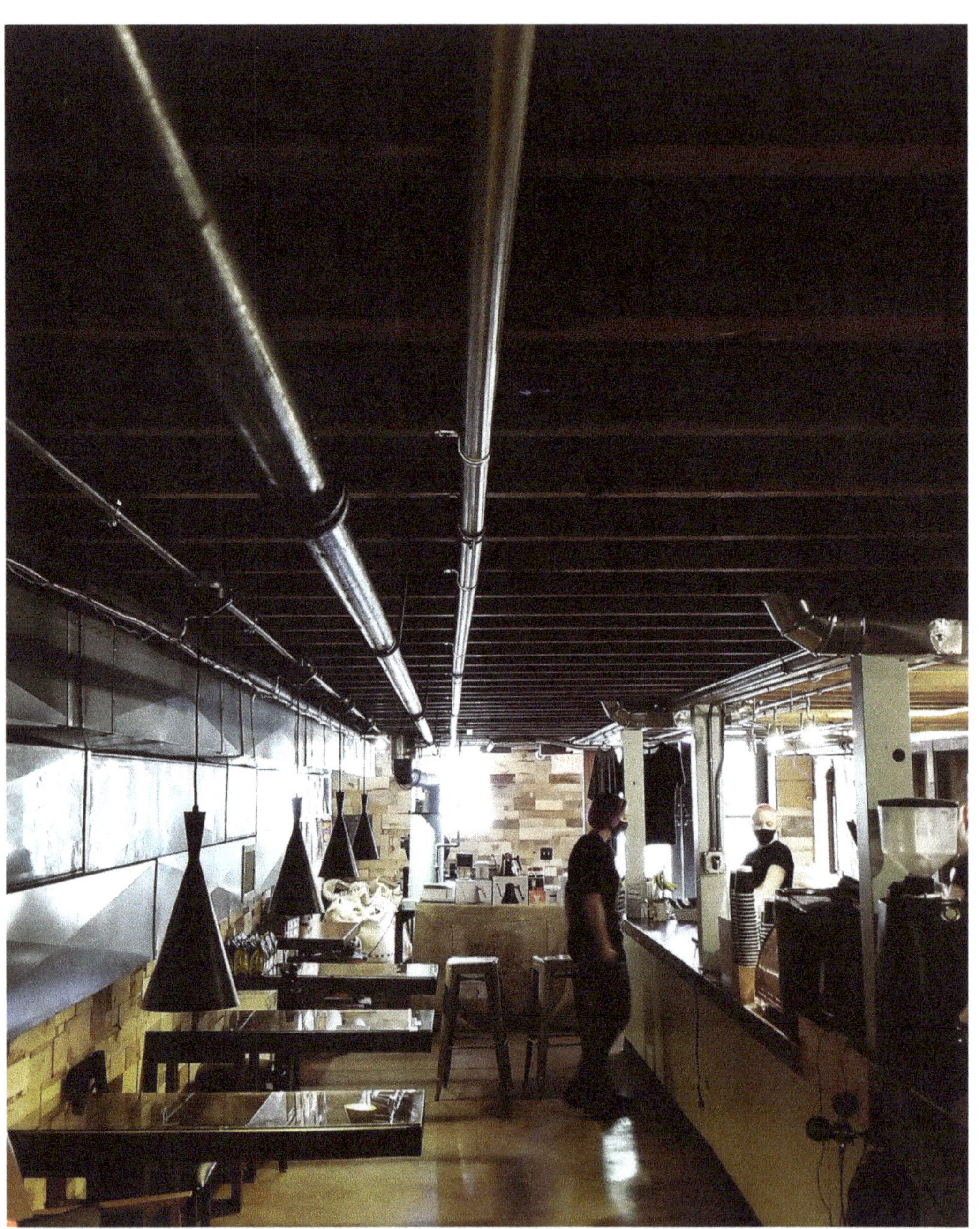

COFFEE COMA

poems & photos about our
love affair & life with coffee

SHEREE K. NIELSEN

SHANTI ARTS PUBLISHING
BRUNSWICK, MAINE

Coffee Coma

poems & photos about our love affair & life with coffee

Published by Shanti Arts Publishing
Interior and cover design by Shanti Arts Designs

Shanti Arts LLC
193 Hillside Road
Brunswick, Maine 04011
www.shantiarts.com

All photographs are by Sheree K. Nielsen with the exception of the photograph on page 10, taken by Nancy Caraway at Sump Coffee; and the photograph on page 24, taken by Russell Nielsen.
Front cover: *Cappuccino in Succulents*, Upshot Brake Shop, St. Charles, Missouri

Printed in the United States of America

ISBN: 978-1-951651-96-1 (softcover)

Library of Congress Control Number: 2021942416

For my close friends, who appreciate a good cup of coffee
and are willing to meet at a local café
or for a chat on the front porch—
Tina, Nancy, Dena, Frankie, Kim C, and Abby—
let's grab a latte, shall we?

For Russell, who turned me on to my very first cappuccino.

For all the baristas and coffeehouse owners—
your jobs are harder and more skillful than we'll ever know.

Thank you so much!

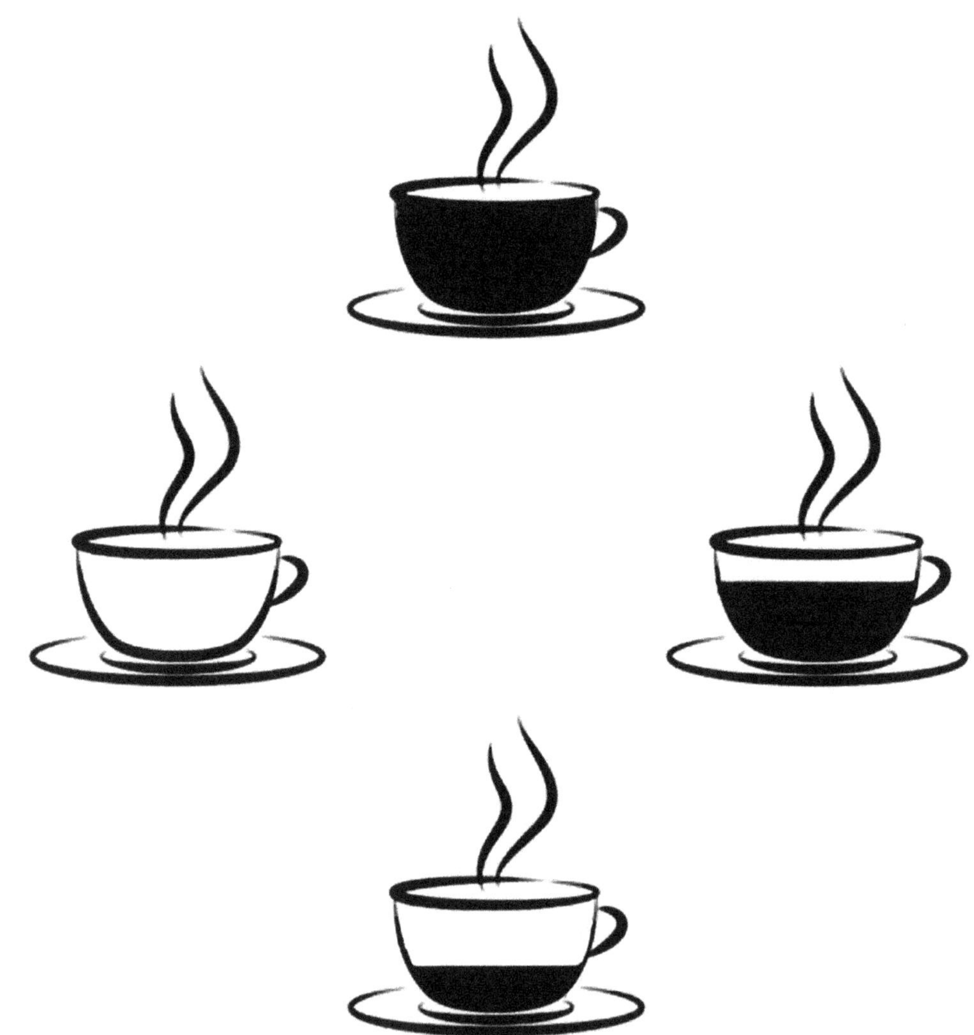

Contents

Notes 9
Introduction 11

Caffeine Addiction 17

Composition
- Roast 20
- Chemistry 22
- Infatuation 24
- Layers 29
- Latte Art 30
- Chaff 32
- Duos 34

Love
- From Granny, with Love 38
- Coffee with Dad 39
- Memories of Mom 40
- Coffee Date 45
- Kiss 47
- Conversation 48

Smile
- Affogato 52
- But First, Coffee 56
- The Jitters 58
- The Keur 61
- Mugs 62
- Don't Cry Over Spilled Coffee 65

Life
- Latte with Friends 69
- Sunday Drive 70
- Coffee with Cats 73
- Morning Coffee 77
- The Drift 79
- Coloring 80
- The Meeting 84
- Going Separate Ways 87
- Coffee Coma 89
- No Caffeine Before Chemo 91
- When I Was Seventeen 92

Sheree's Favorite Coffeehouses 99
About the Author 105

Notes

"Kiss" was first published in *Book of Matches: A Literary Journal*, Issue 2, May 1, 2021; and "Kiss" won First Place for Poetry in the St. Louis Writers Guild, Deane Wagner Poetry Contest 2020.

"Coffee with Cats" won an Honorable Mention for Poetry in the St. Louis Writers Guild, Deanne Wagner Poetry Contest 2020.

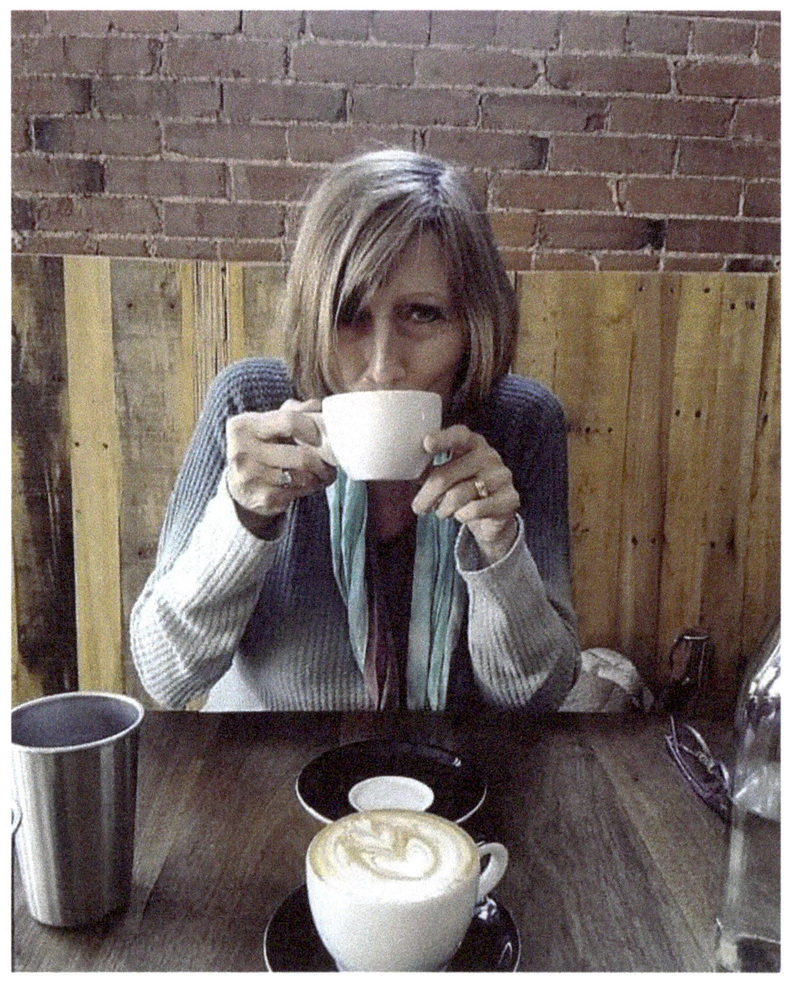

Introduction

When I think about my relationship with coffee, I can say we've been simpatico for many years. A good friend, coffee is always around no matter the situation, location, or weather.

Don't get me wrong. For years, I loved tea as much as coffee. Every day, and for as far back as I can remember, I would steep tea for breakfast, but coffee kept me moving and focused as I planned my day.

Today, I love a latte with friends to catch up on news or an iced cappuccino while I'm running errands. An espresso does just fine when I'm listening to jazz or folk music at a café. From my front porch, a light roast satisfies while admiring a mango-hued sun dipping below the horizon or the fireflies' luminescence lighting up the night.

I guess my love of coffee began at age seventeen. On a camping trip, I rummaged through the RV's kitchen cabinets, searching for tea bags. Unable to find them, I just about lost my mind.

"Where's the tea?!" I yelled.

"All we have is coffee," my friend replied.

In the company of kindred spirits, we gathered around a blazing fire. I sipped coffee from an indigo blue enamelware mug . . . and it tasted good.

Five years later, my fondness for the liquid energy came to a halt. Diagnosed with a serious medical condition at age twenty-two, at my doctor's advice–no caffeine. I'd cheat on occasion, but for the most part, I cut out coffee for the next sixteen years.

Until . . . I met my second husband, who easily consumed four to five cups of coffee within a couple hours. In addition to a coffee maker, he owned a shiny espresso machine that rested regally on his kitchen countertop.

"May I make you a cappuccino?" Russell asked on one of our first dates.

"Yes, please."

We became connected by coffee almost immediately. He wasn't a bad kisser either.

When a coffeehouse opened about a half mile from our house, we jumped for joy. On the weekends we'd flock to Picasso's whose credo was "the art of coffee." Unique art filled the walls of the café, conversation flowed, and the lattes were yummy. Picasso's was the place to be.

Decades later, while out with twenty-something friends, we headed to

Picasso's on historic Main Street—their second location. The line of people waiting to get inside spilled onto the sidewalk.

"What do we do now?"

Danielle, our young friend suggested, "Let's go to VB's in Cottleville!"

"What's VB's?'

"It's ONLY the best kept secret in town."

Nearing our destination, we motored down quaint streets and steered our vehicle into a parking lot where an unassuming buttercream-hued ranch building came into view. Stepping inside, the atmosphere was inviting—baristas smiled, twinkling lights hung from the rafters, and weathered greige tables with mismatched chairs filled the café. In addition to coffee selections, a glass case of homemade ice creams enticed as well as a selection of artisanal chocolates. Coffee, chocolate, and ice cream—you can't beat that combination.

I was hooked.

VB's Chocolate Bar, now Upshot Coffee, became my retreat to create, write, be inspired. The café's warm ambiance felt like home. At the time, I even managed to convince my editor for a Missouri magazine they needed a food review of the cool establishment.

Today, when planning vacations, I check to ensure there's a recommended coffeehouse nearby. Even better—a local roaster; then I'm almost guaranteed the coffee is going to be fantastic.

Picasso's and VB's set the standard of quality for me early on. I became—a coffee snob.

My sense of taste would be knocked down temporarily. Mid-November 2018, I began chemotherapy for Waldenstrom's macroglobulinemia. After each treatment, impaired taste lasted for up to ten days. So much for coffee.

Heading home from Christmas at my in-laws, I craved coffee. In the pouring rain, my husband navigated the Chevy Equinox fifteen minutes off course to the best dang coffeehouse in downtown Clarksville, Tennessee. Locally owned, Plumb Line Coffee was an artisanal coffee café near Peay State University. Walking through the door, I perused the board with the coffee offerings and ordered a vanilla latte. With the first sip, I was infatuated—so rich and velvety.

In spring of 2020, before social distancing was in full swing, I planned a short getaway to Ocean Springs, Mississippi. A charming town with shaded streets, cute boutiques, and farm-to-table restaurants, it was home to Bright-Eyed Brew. The coffeehouse, owned by the Reaux family, served the best coffee around. The teeny café became our morning stop before exploring nearby beach towns. The pups loved it too. Katherine Reaux won them over with daily doggie treats. Garnering a seat at a cozy table on the shady side porch, we became skillful at people watching and learning to slow down.

Back home, with cafés closed due to the Covid-19 restrictions, we ordered Bright-Eyed Brew online, shipped directly to our door.

Recently, my husband taught me the art of pulling espresso shots on the De Longhi. I think I've become pretty adept at this skill, and I look forward to making my morning latte every day.

Coffee is always forefront in my mind and is the foundation for my collection, *Coffee Coma: Poems & Photos about Our Love Affair & Life with Coffee.*

I hope you enjoy the different sections of the book: Composition, Love, Life, and Smile. I had a blast creating the poems and selecting the photographs . . . so many of coffee! There's also a listing at the back of my favorite coffeehouses around the country–and one in the Caribbean. These places have strengthened my appreciation of coffee, especially Course Coffee Roasters in St. Charles and Long Row Lavender in Wright City, Missouri.

Please feel free to share your favorite coffeehouses or coffee recipes with me on any of my social media platforms, or contact me at www.shereenielsen.wordpress.com.

Life is an adventure.
Get out and go find a coffeehouse!

Peace, Love, and Coffee,

Sheree

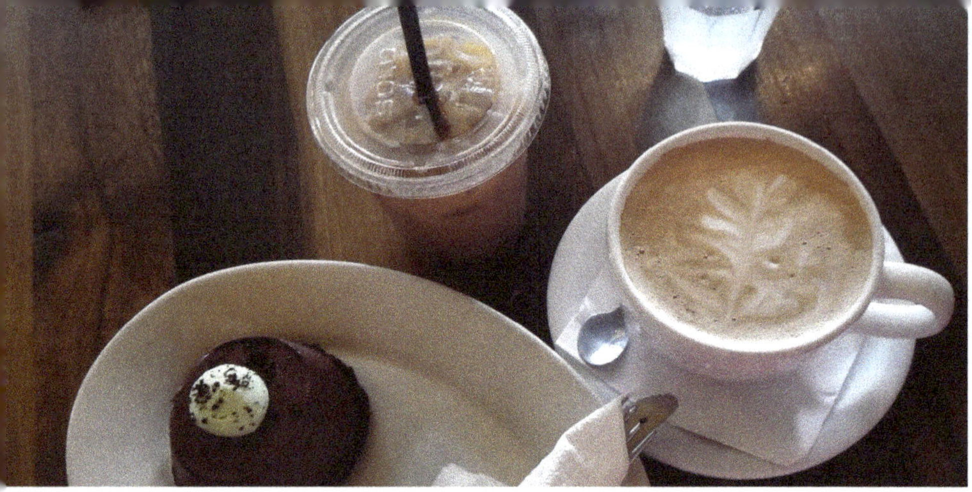

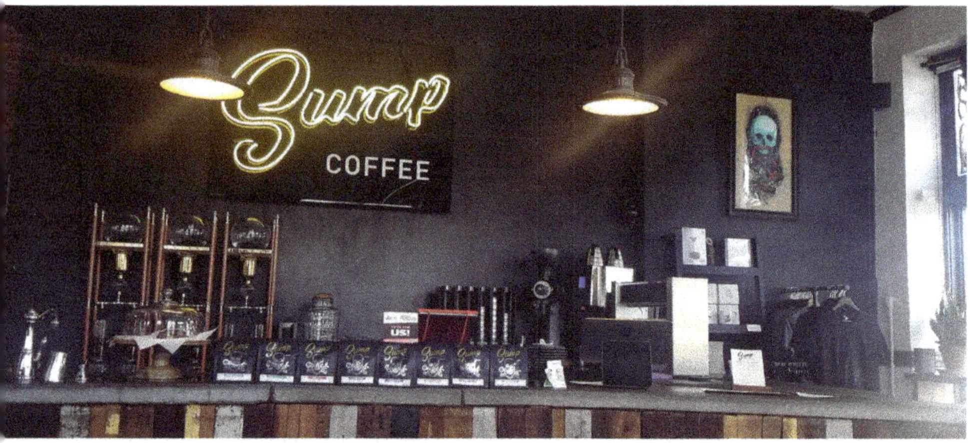

Sump
COFFEE
EST. 2019 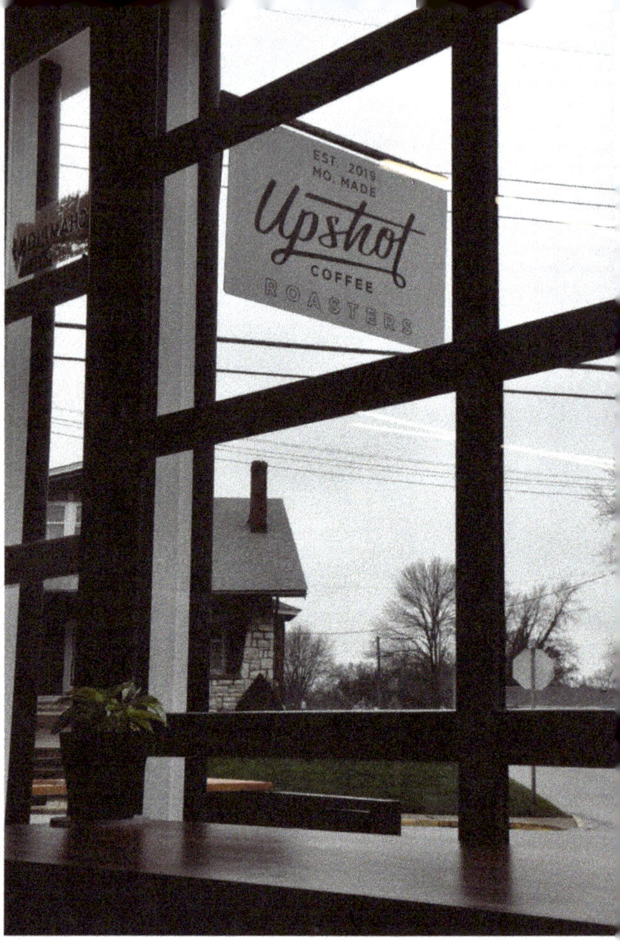
MO. MADE
Upshot
COFFEE
ROASTERS
SUNERGOS COFFEE

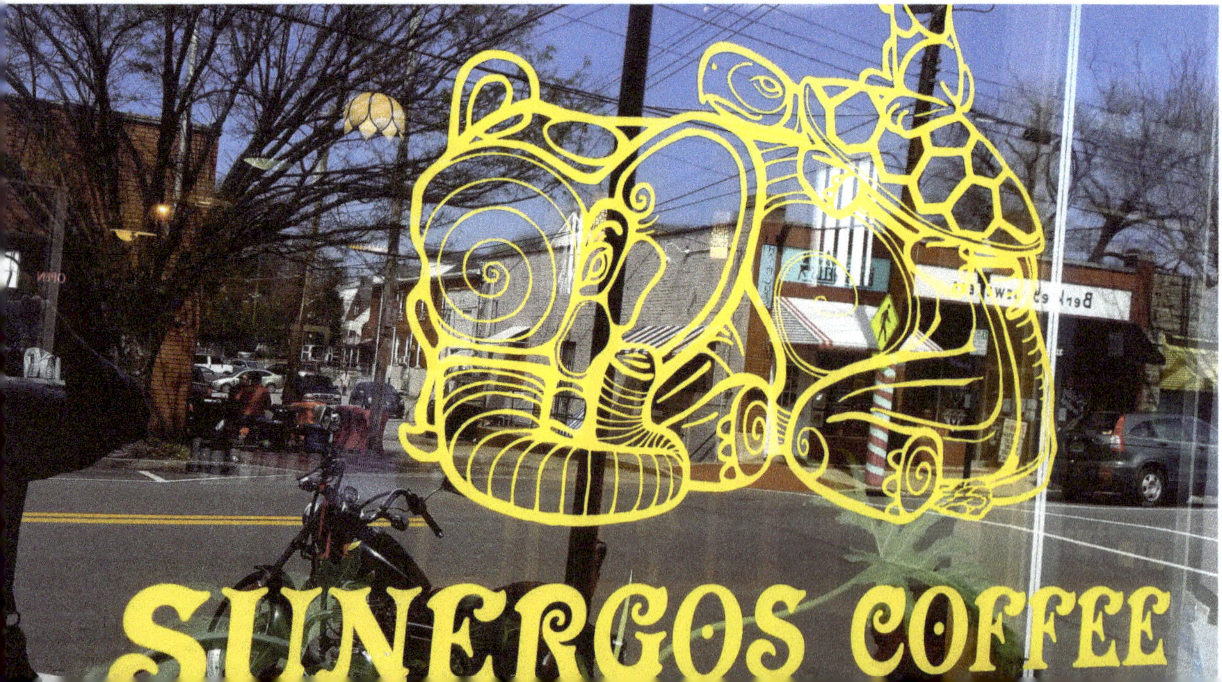

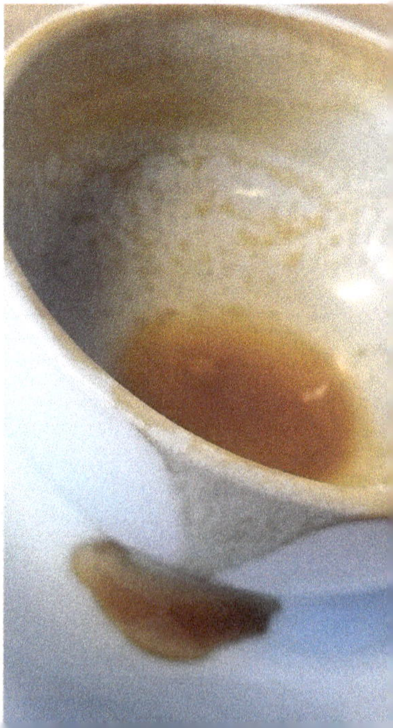

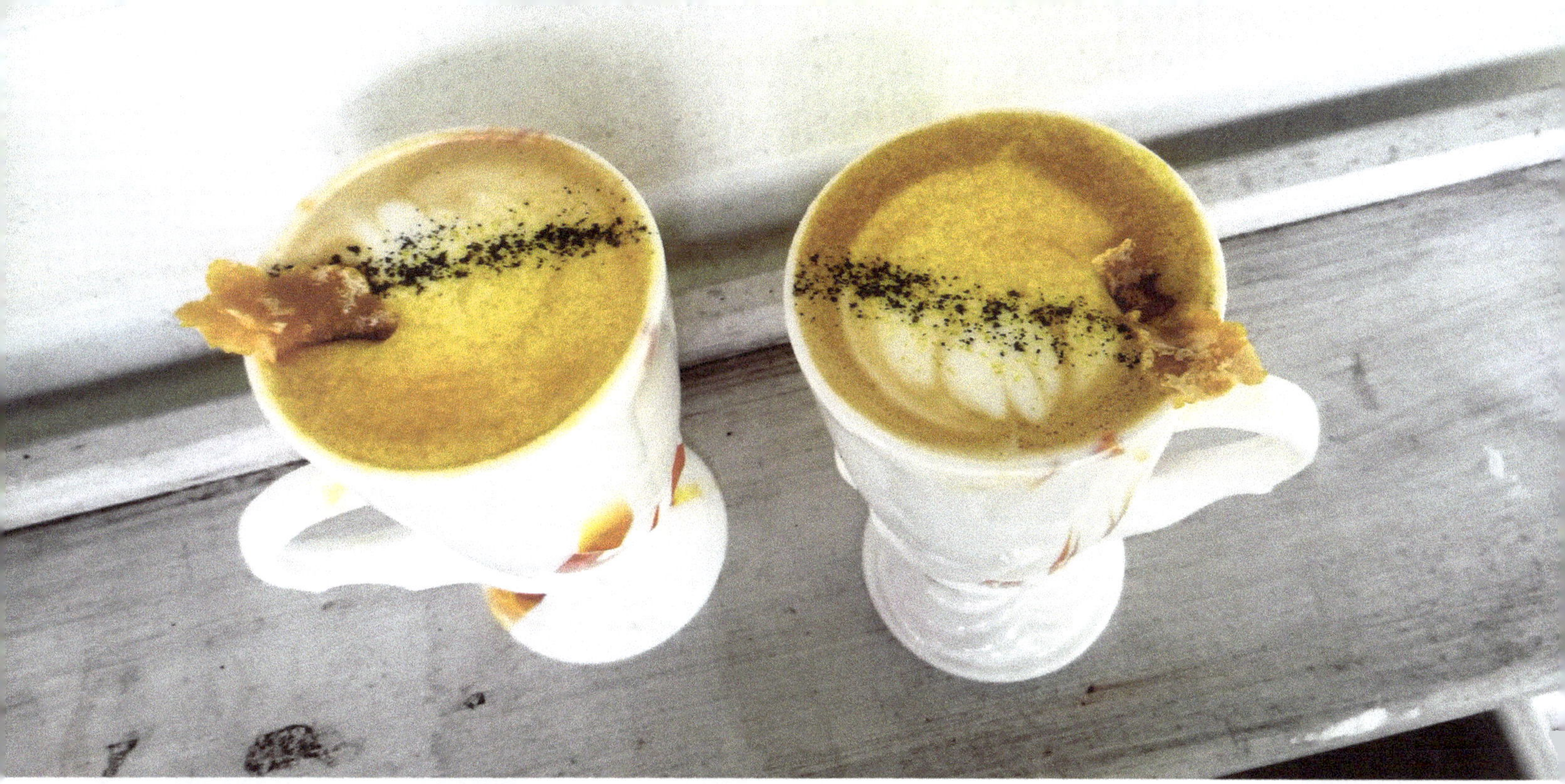

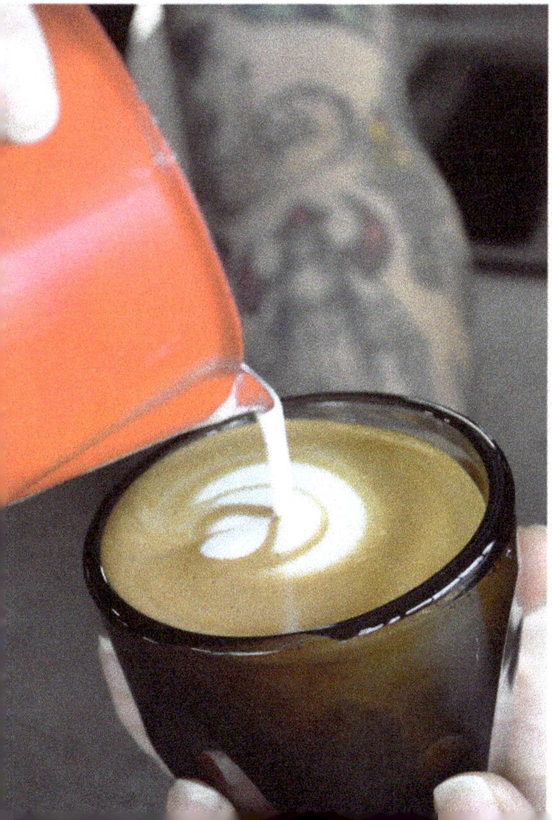

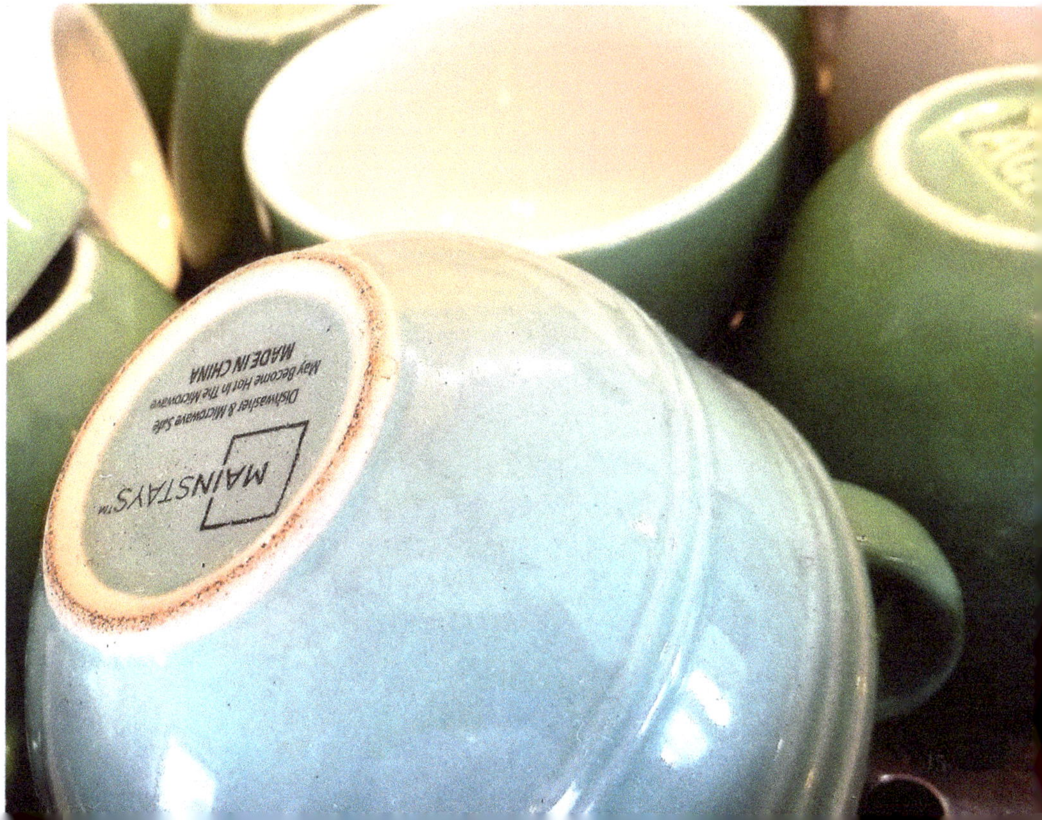

MAINSTAYS™
Dishwasher & Microwave Safe
May Become Hot In The Microwave
MADE IN CHINA

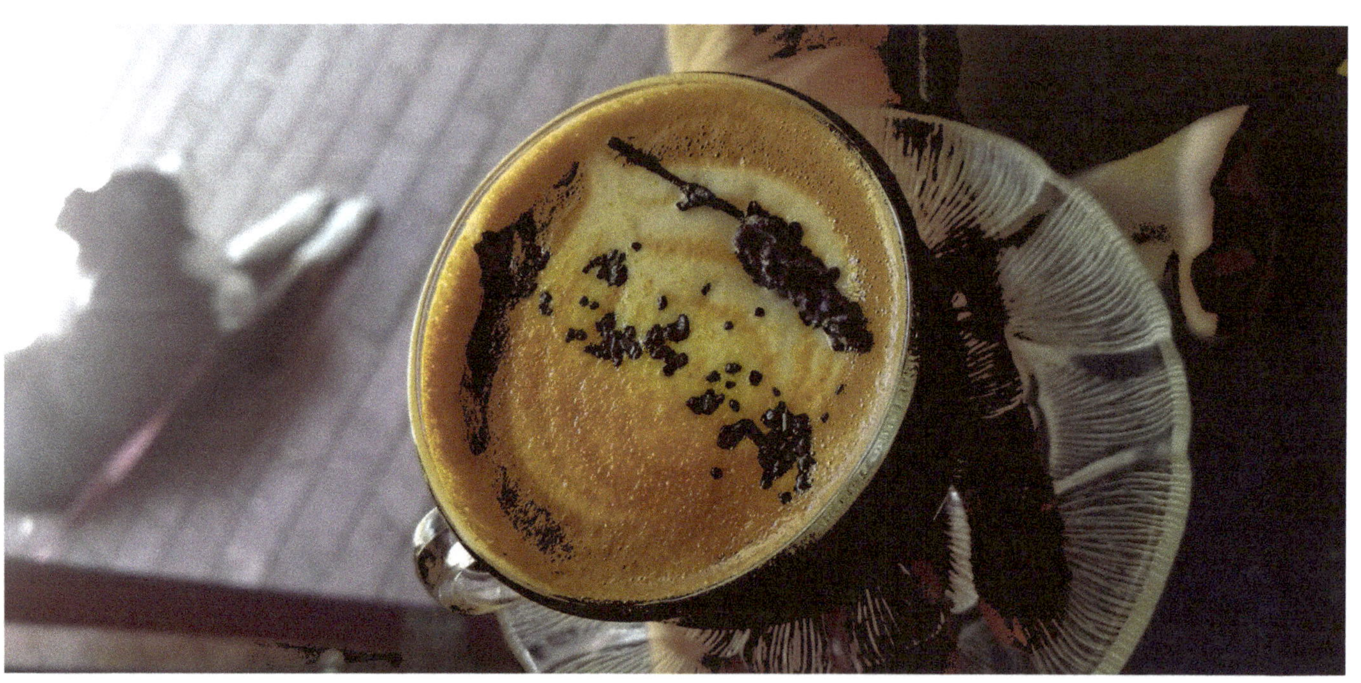

Caffeine Addiction

The practice of planning events, activities or vacation around preferred coffeehouse locations.

Composition

Roast

I'm a medium
roast kind of
gal.

He's a light
roast kind
of guy.

Together
we crack.

But one
tolerates the heat
a little
longer.

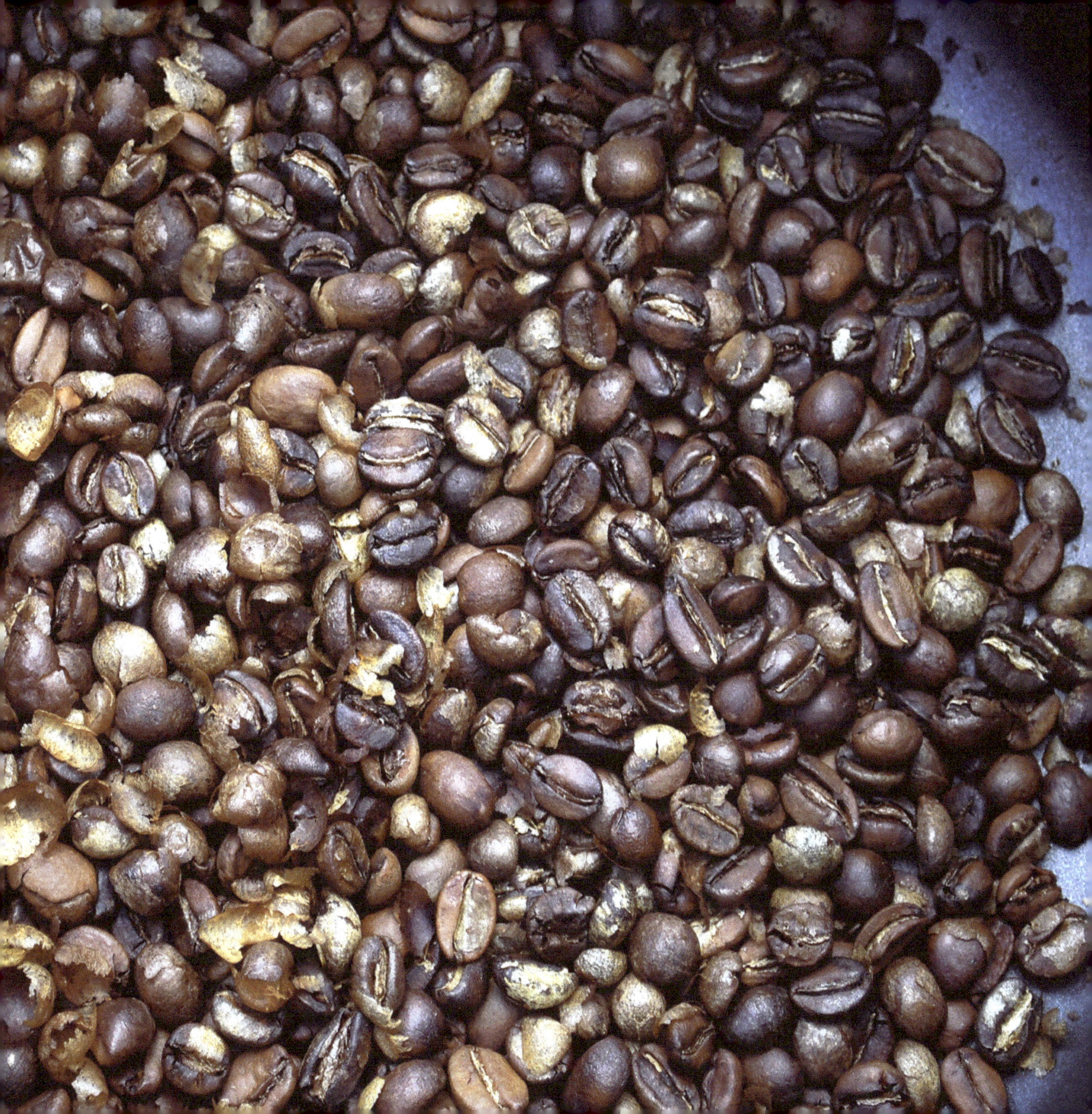

Chemistry

Caffeine–

Is it
your molecular compatibility
that makes me
want you?

You stimulate me
without asking
for a
commitment.

I'm
addicted
to your
adrenaline rush.

My heart beats
faster
when you're
near.

And just like
the honeybee,
lilac
smells sweeter
after
I've imbibed
in your
velvety nectar.

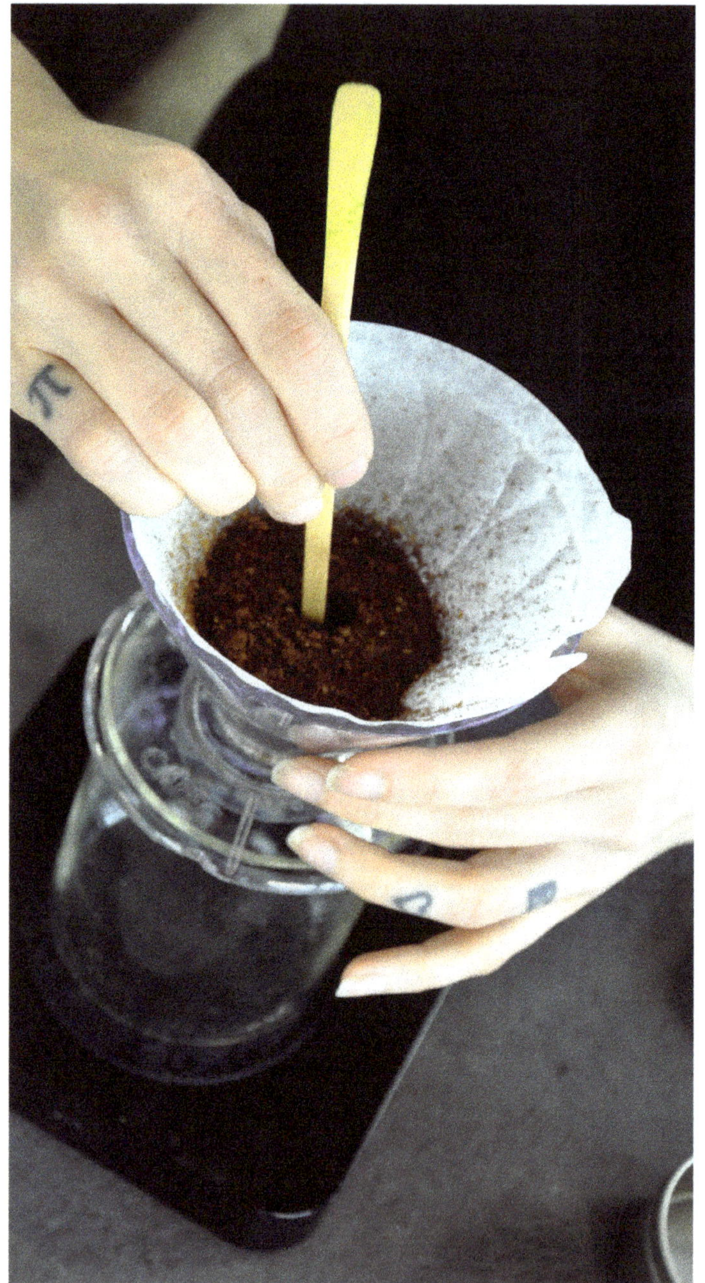

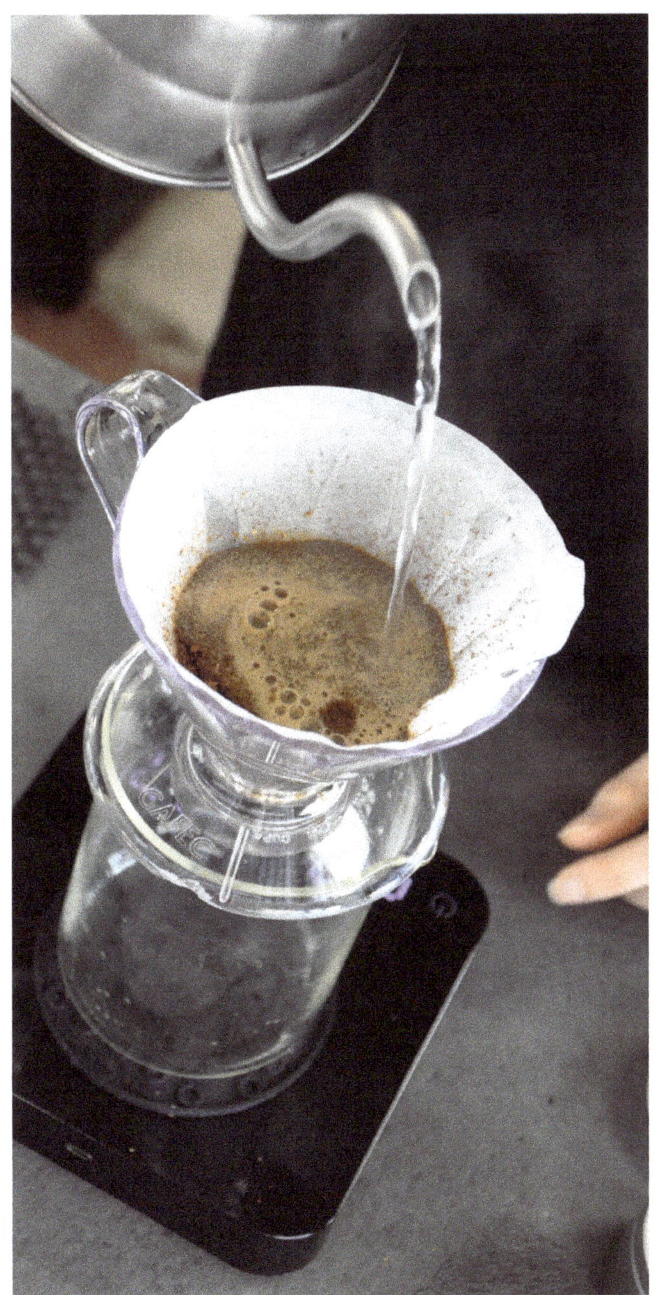

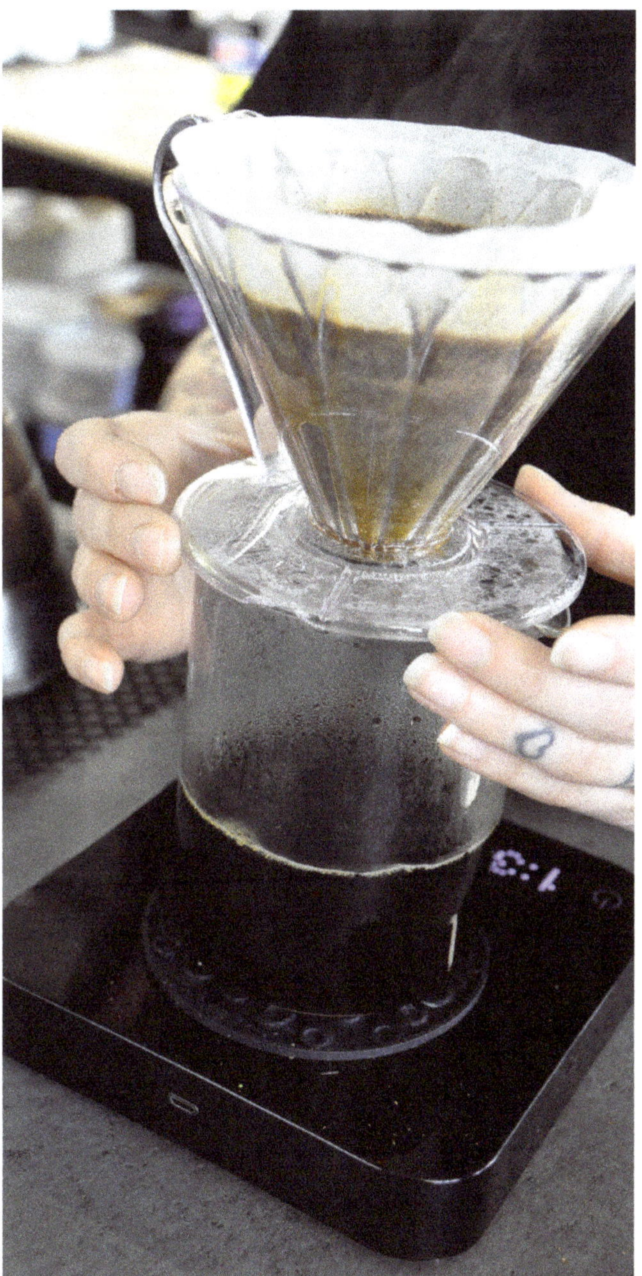

Infatuation

Coffee.
You had me
at
Grind.

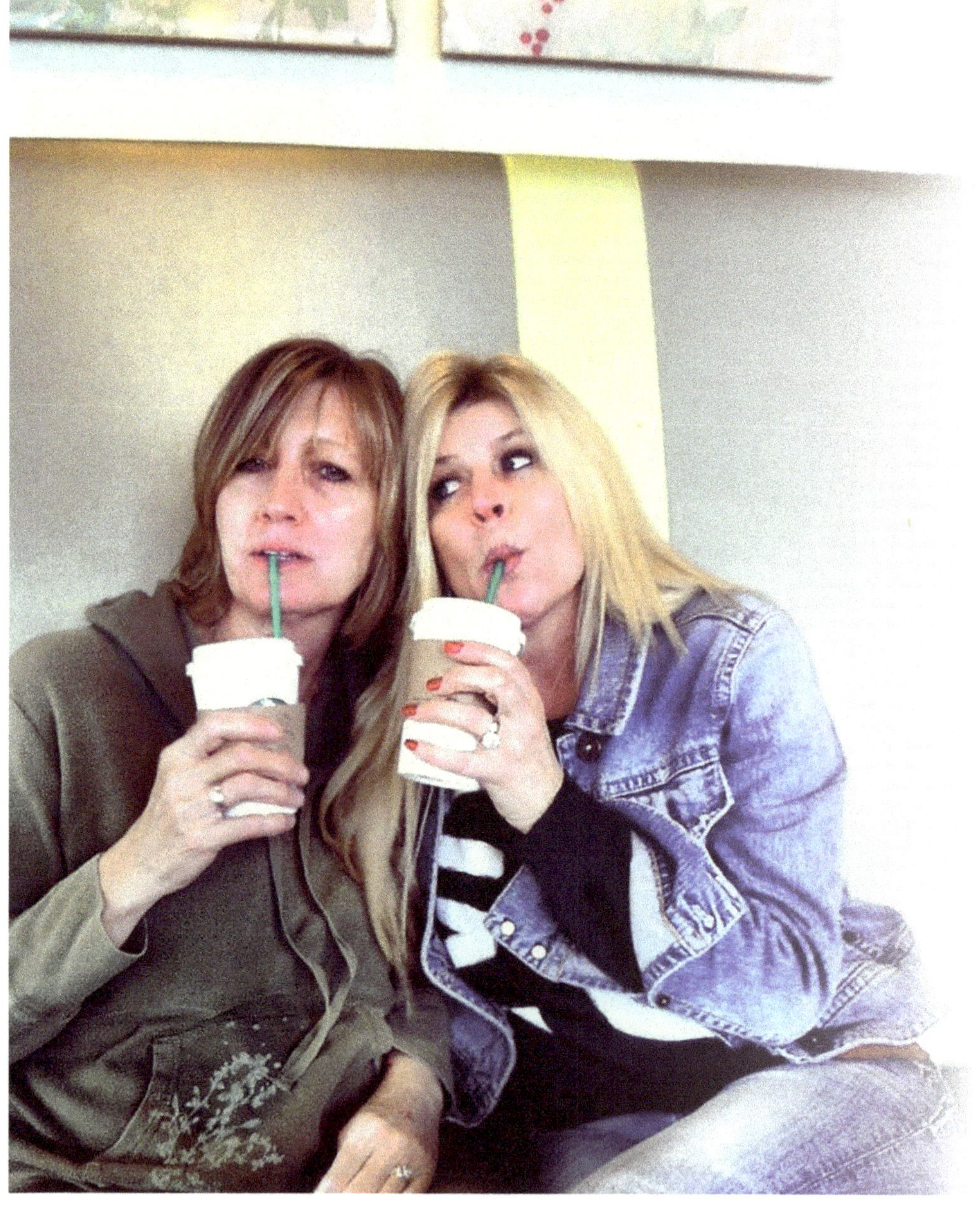

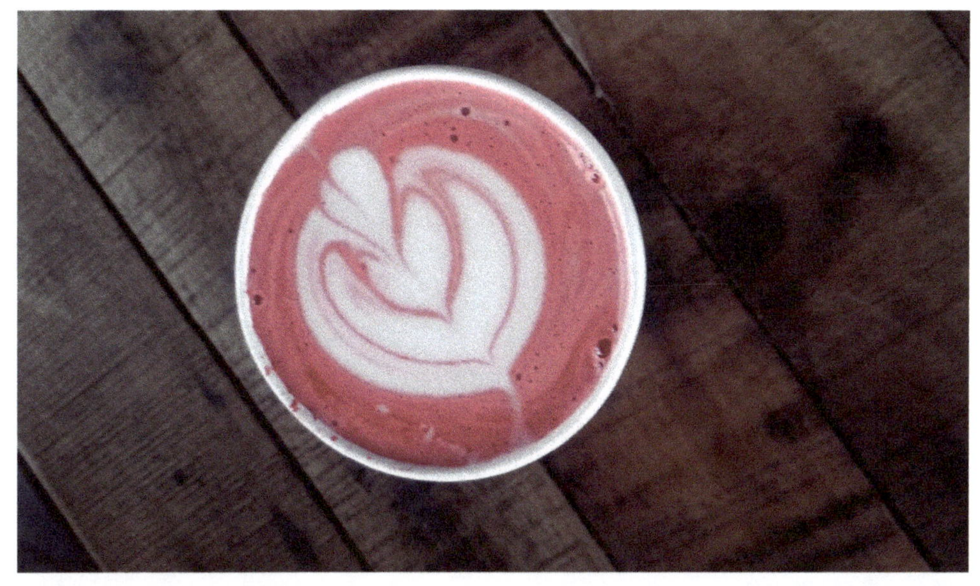

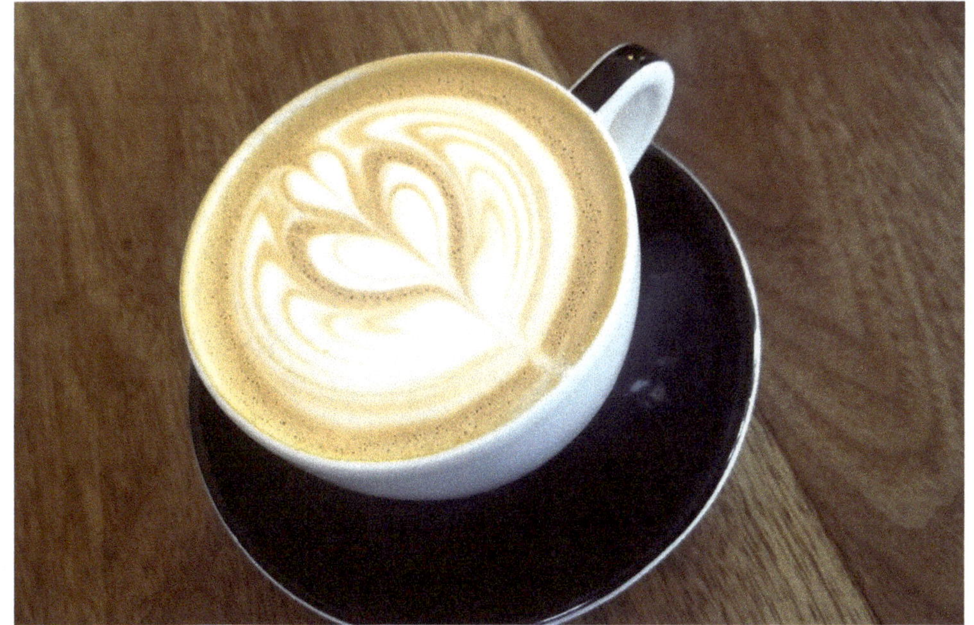

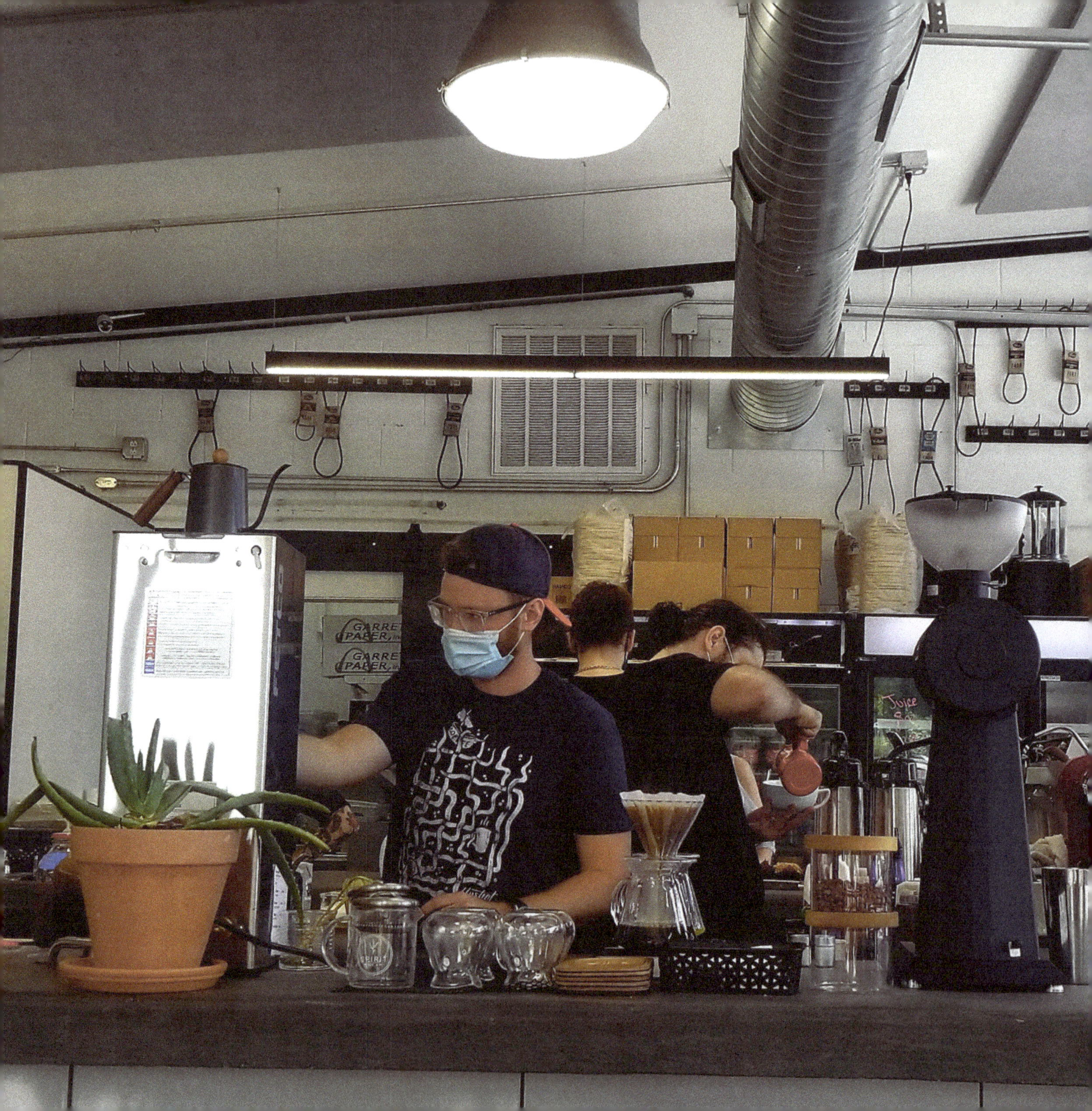

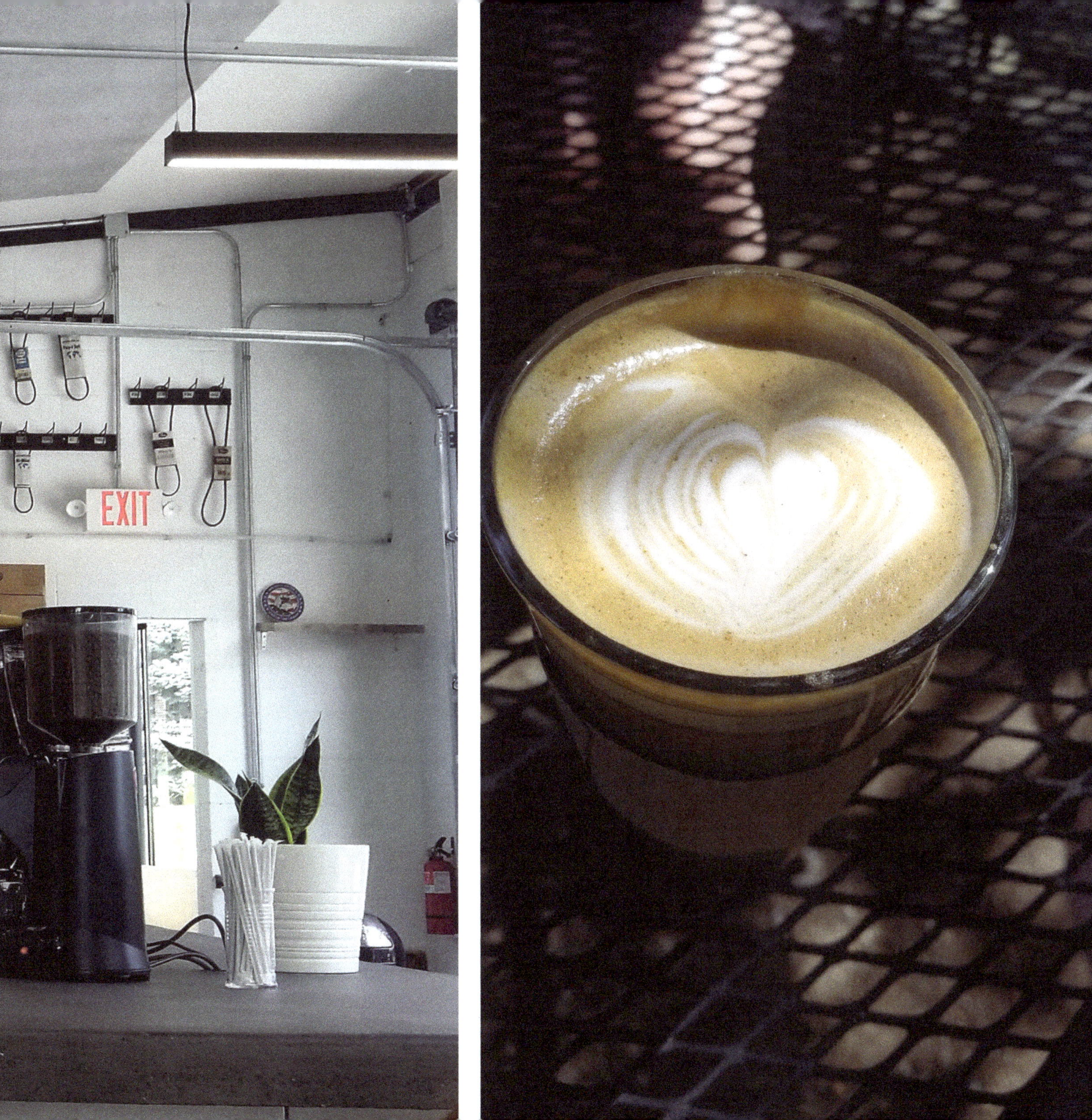
EXIT

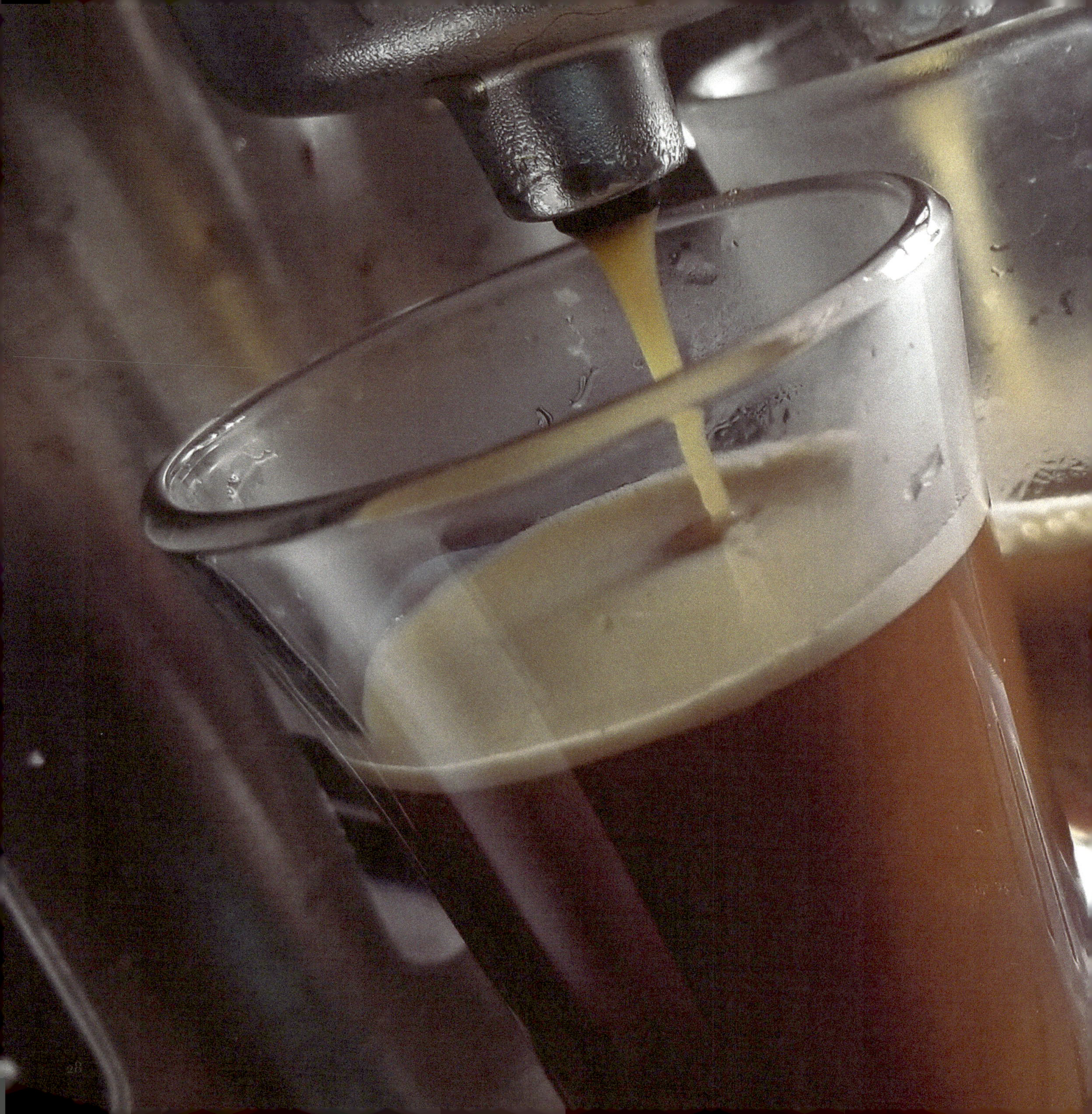

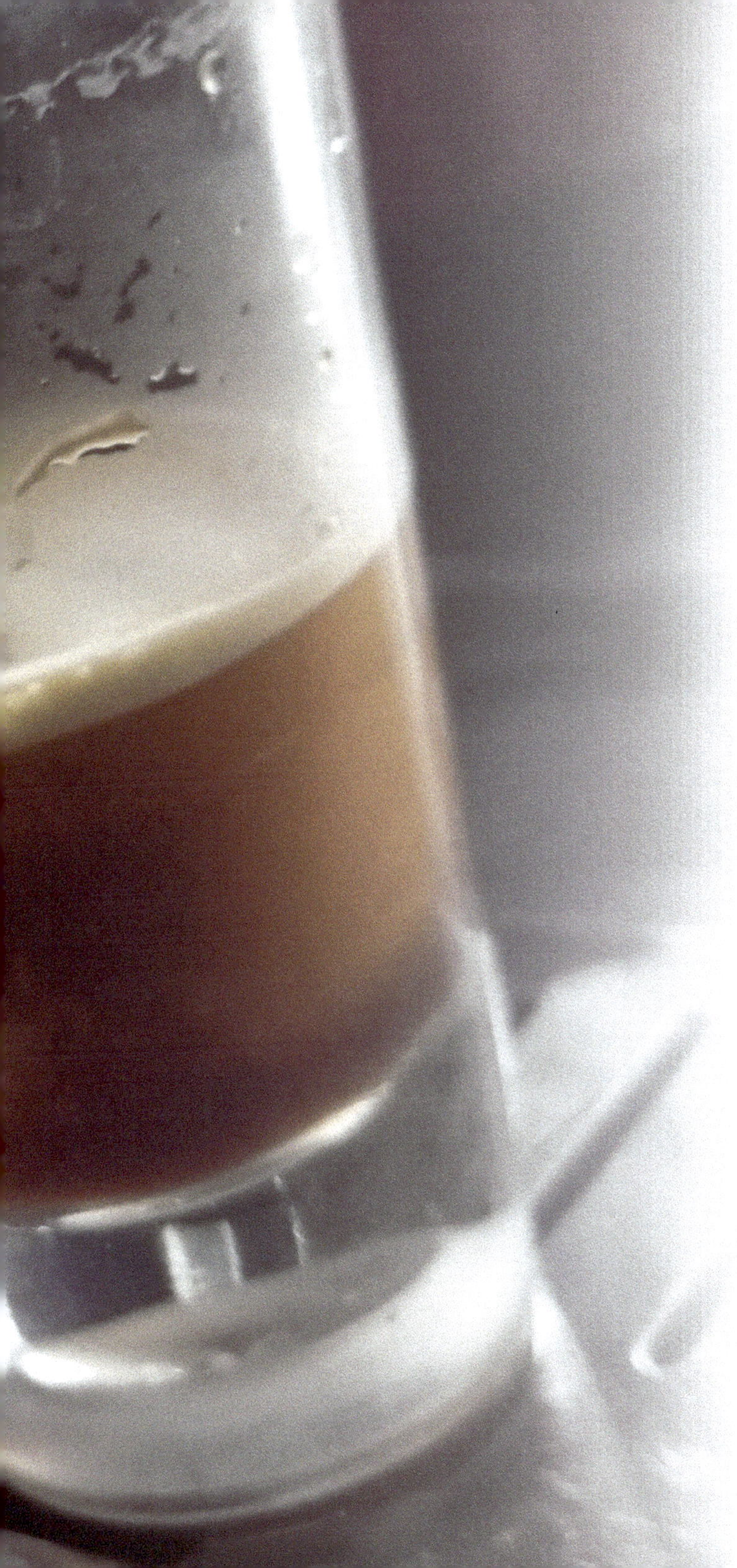

Layers

In the beginning,
There's heart, filled with soul,
balance and spirit.
A home base.
That comfortable feeling . . .

In the middle, there's body
based on substance, feel, and
physicality.

Finally, there's crema–
lovely, light, and frothy

Together they effect
the sweetest taste.

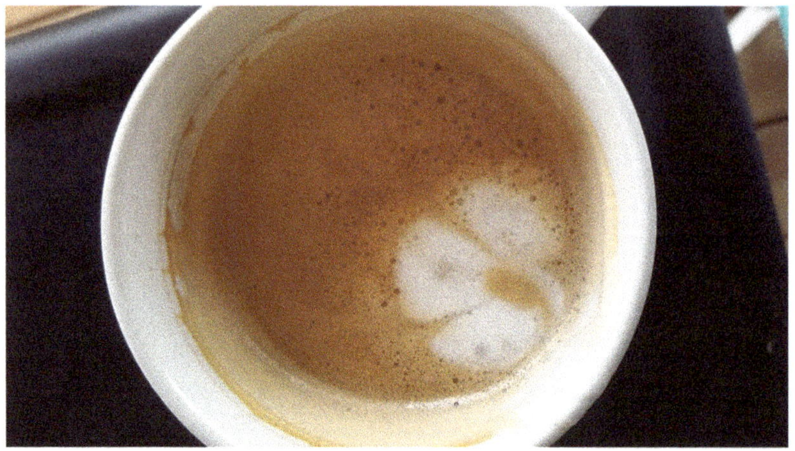

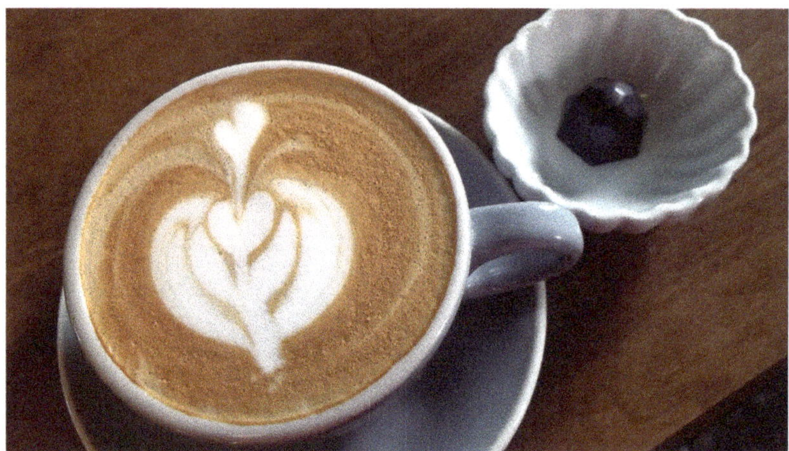

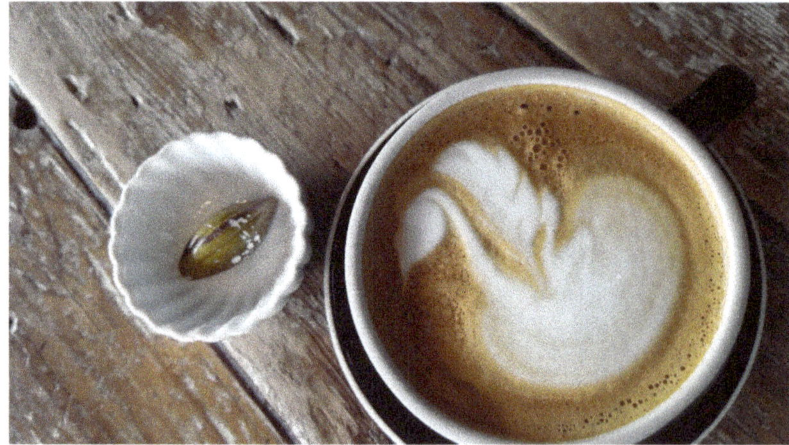

Latte Art

Whisk me away
to a sea of butterscotch
where lily white swans,
whimsical dragons,
and delightful dolphins
swim,
tulips and four-leaf clover
bloom,
Rosetta vines
proliferate,
waves and storm's eye
whirl,
wings soar high
above the toffee
ocean,
and hearts
are good
to the last
drop.

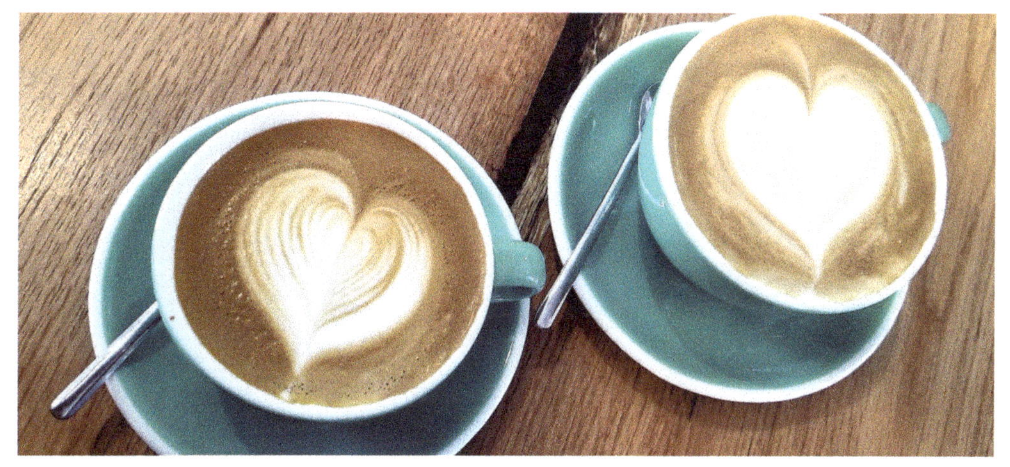

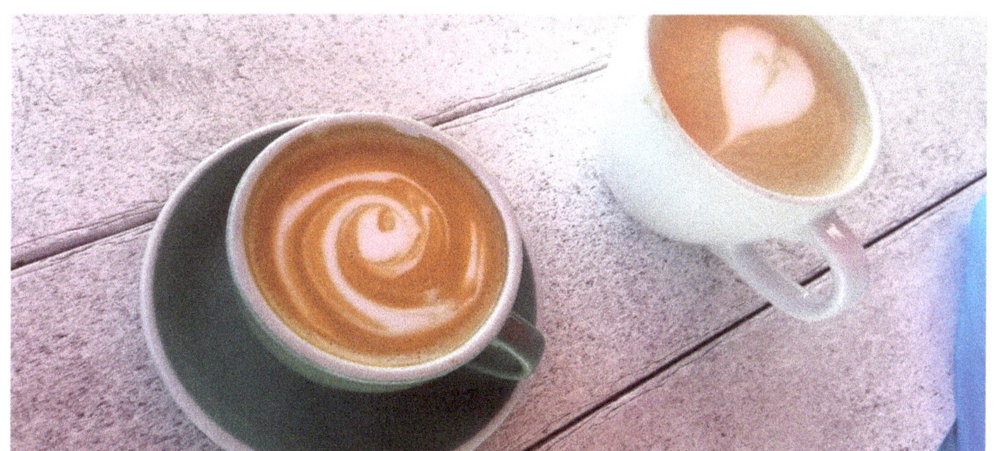

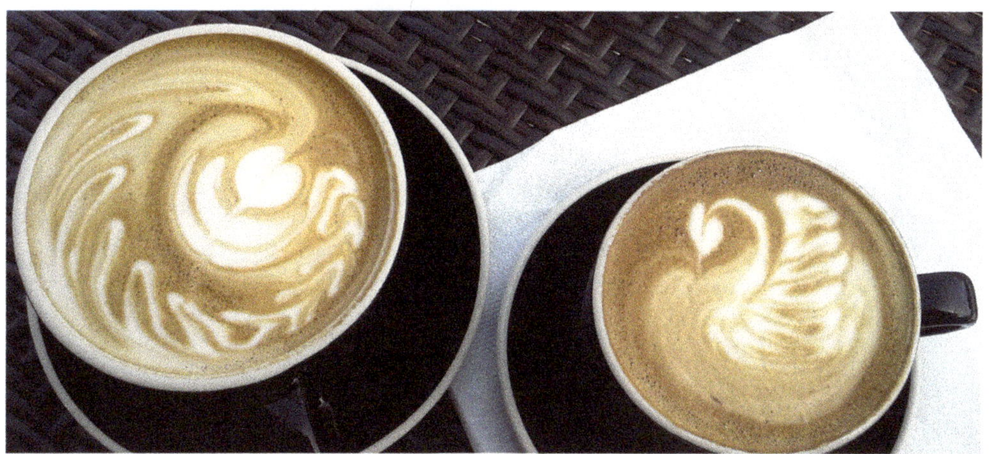

Chaff

Although you come across
with a tough outer
skin,
your light and airy
presence
is revealed
in delicate snowflakes
filling up the space
all around
me.

You are necessary!

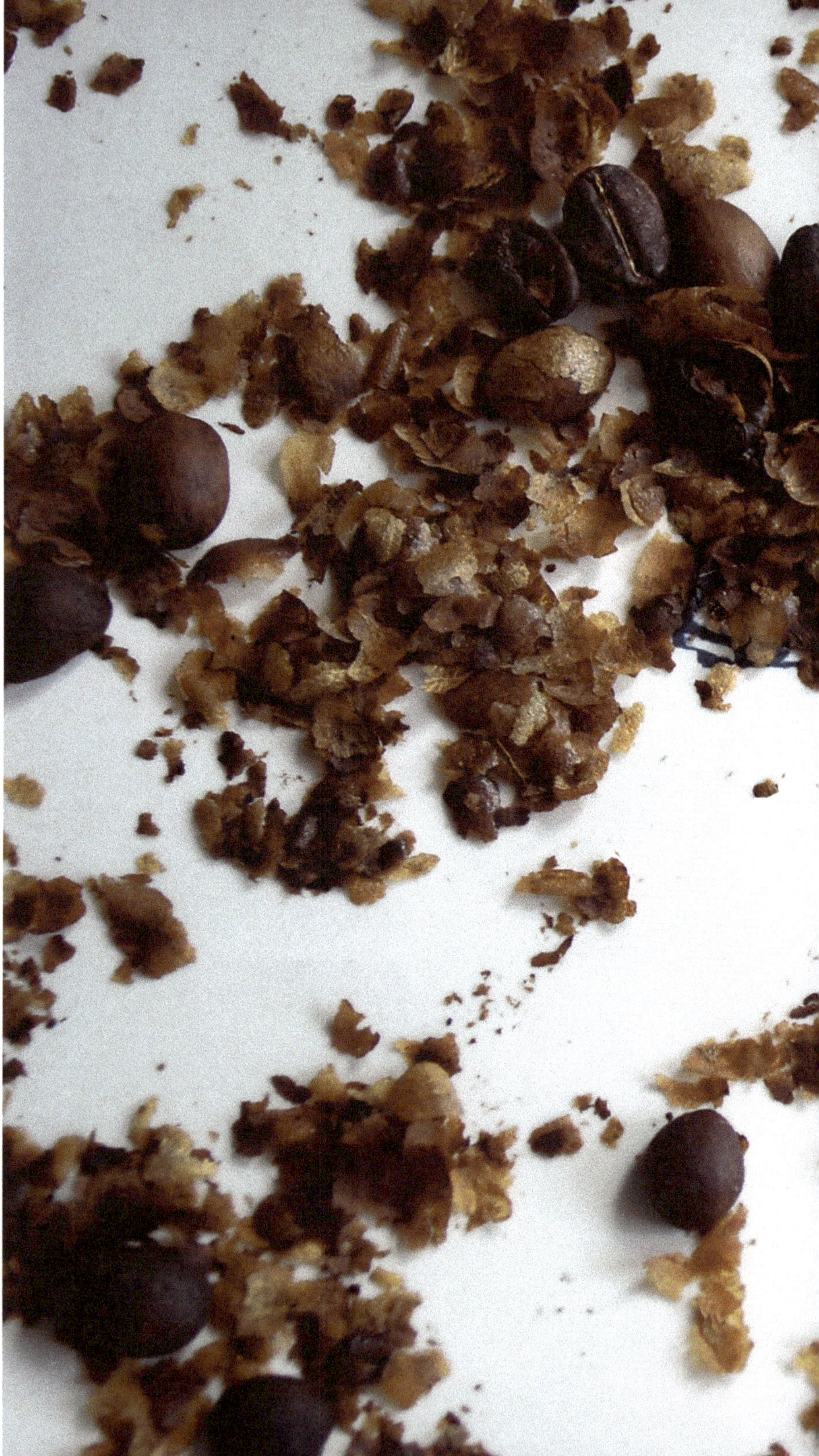

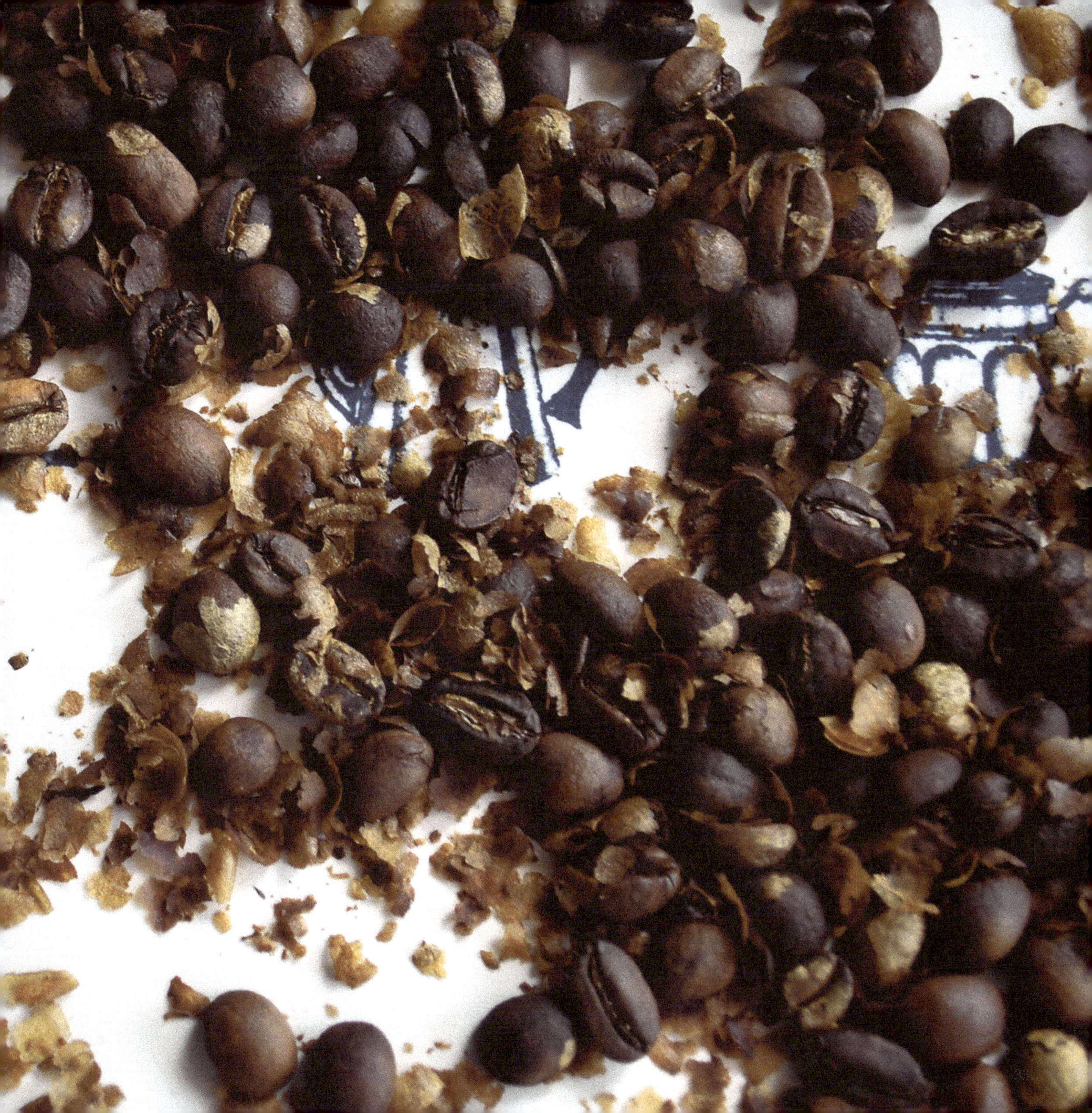

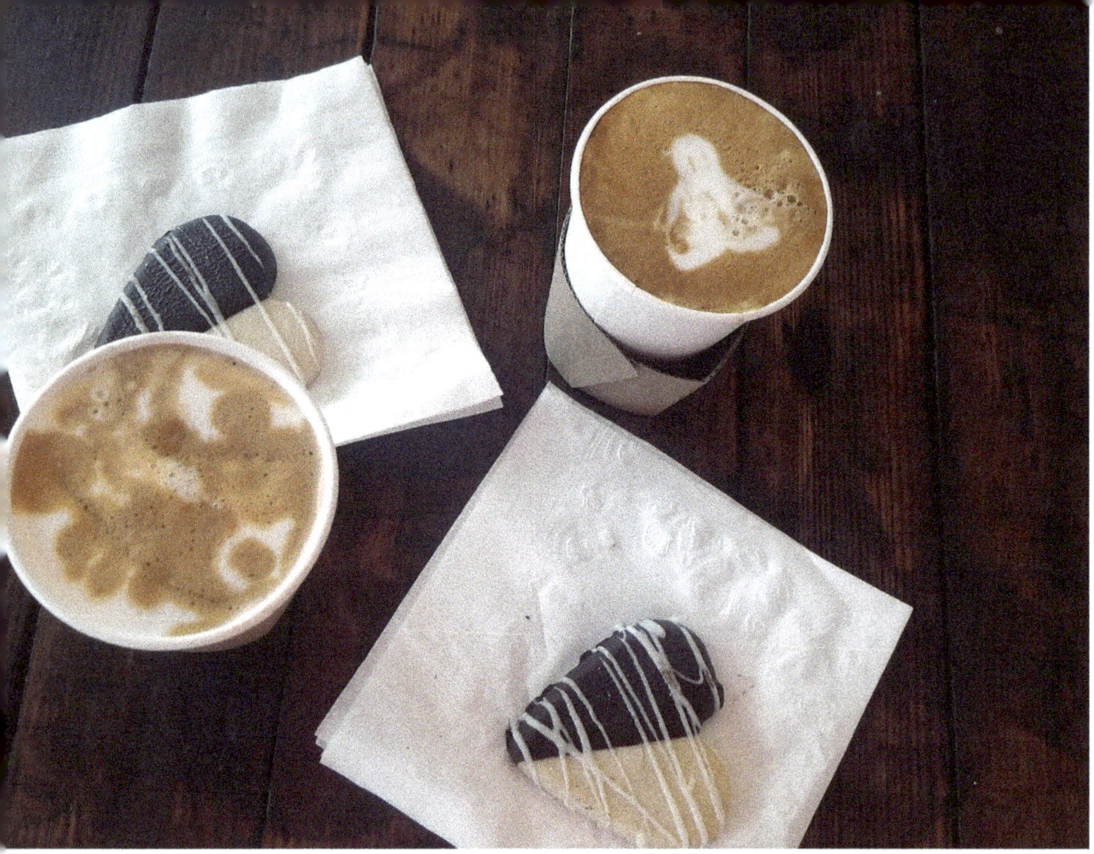

Duos

Some things are just better together
like chocolate and coffee

The perfect union
of bitter and sweet . . .

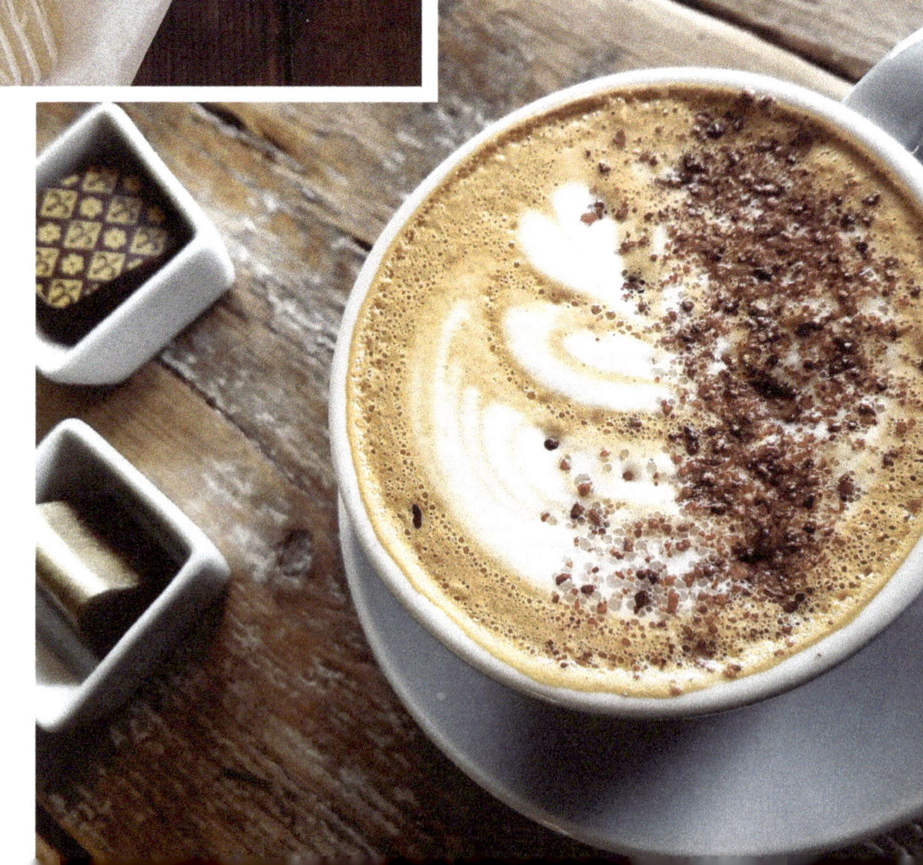

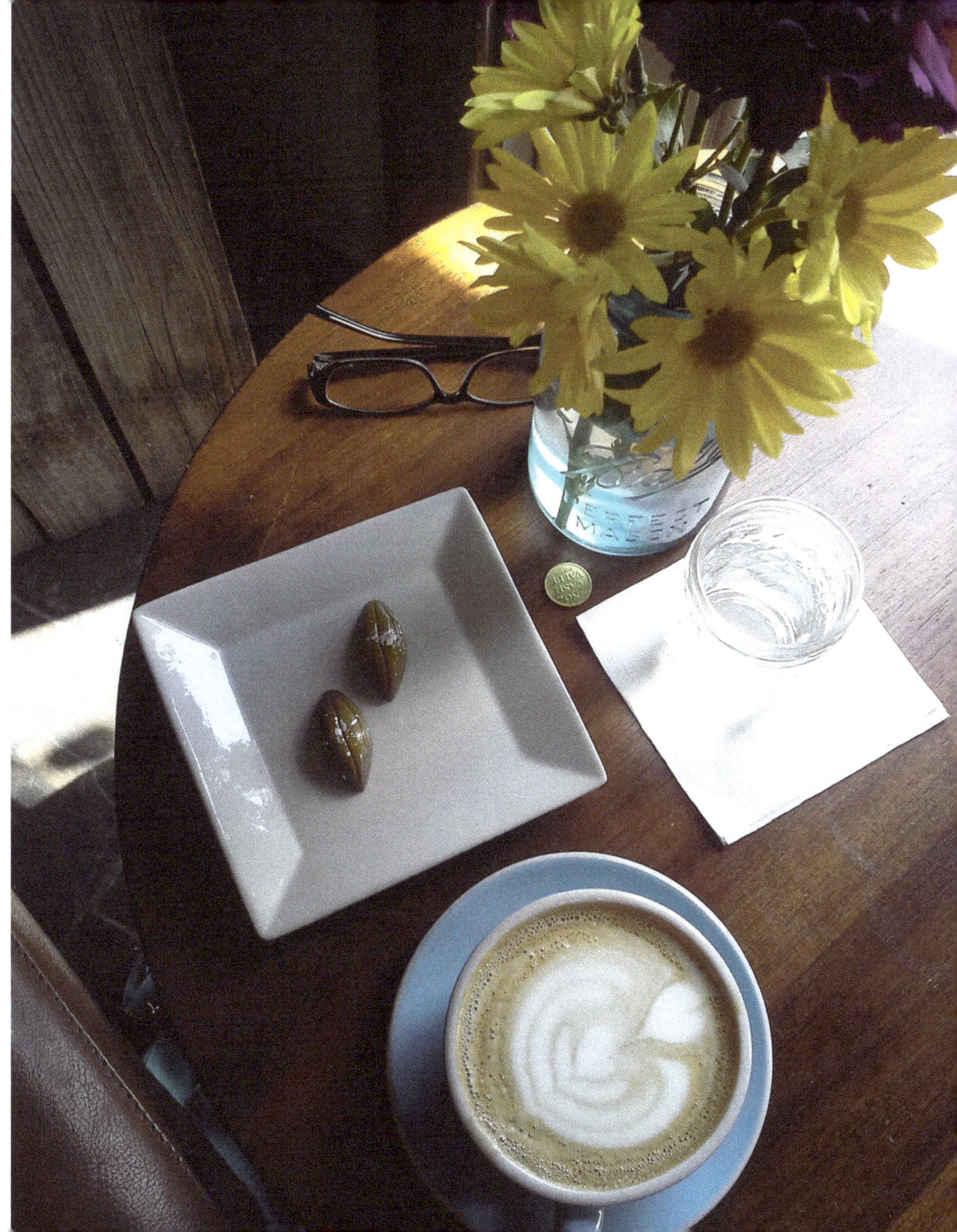

Love

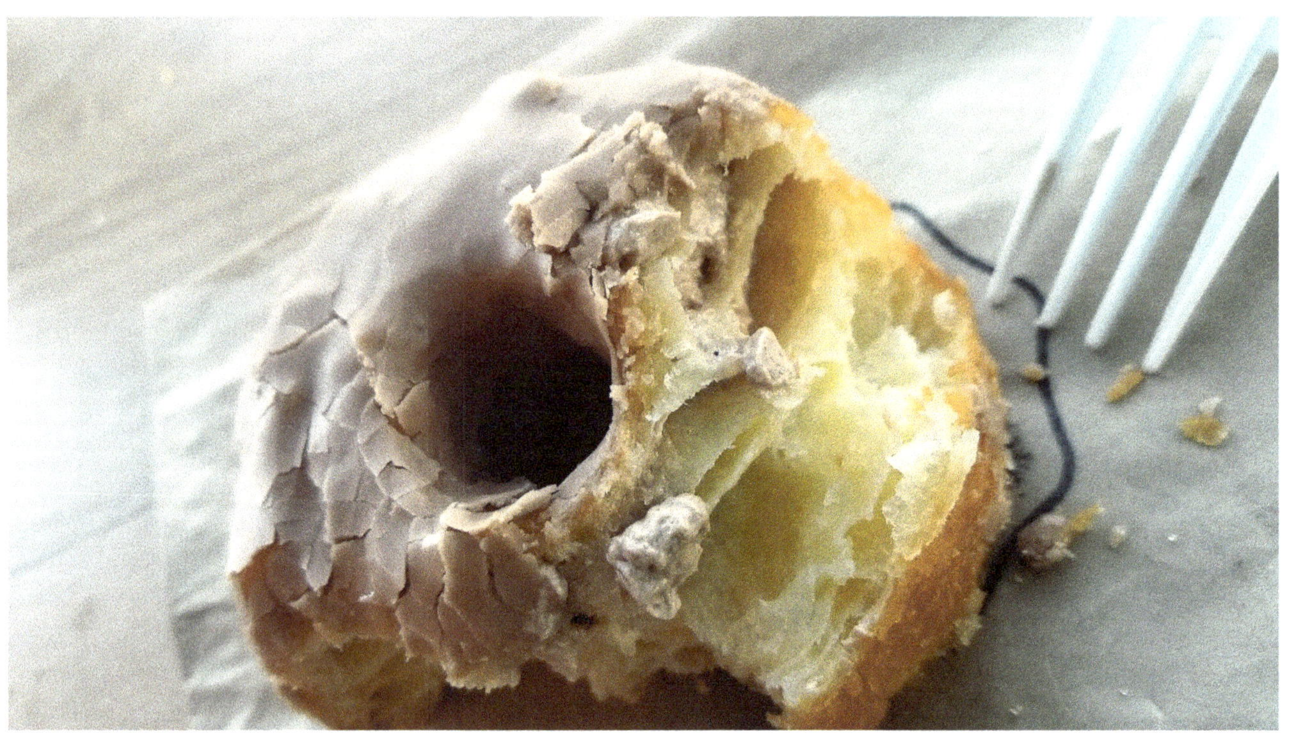

From Granny, with Love

Granny
stirs with love and mixes well
an ample amount
of cream and sugar
to a wee bit of coffee.

Perfect for dunking
buttered toast,
warm chocolate chip cookies,
and even
stale
donuts.

Coffee with Dad

The pleasant aroma
of brew
simmers and gurgles
in the shiny metal
percolator and teases
my nostril tips,
in anticipation of Dad
and mornings,
in the house that built me.

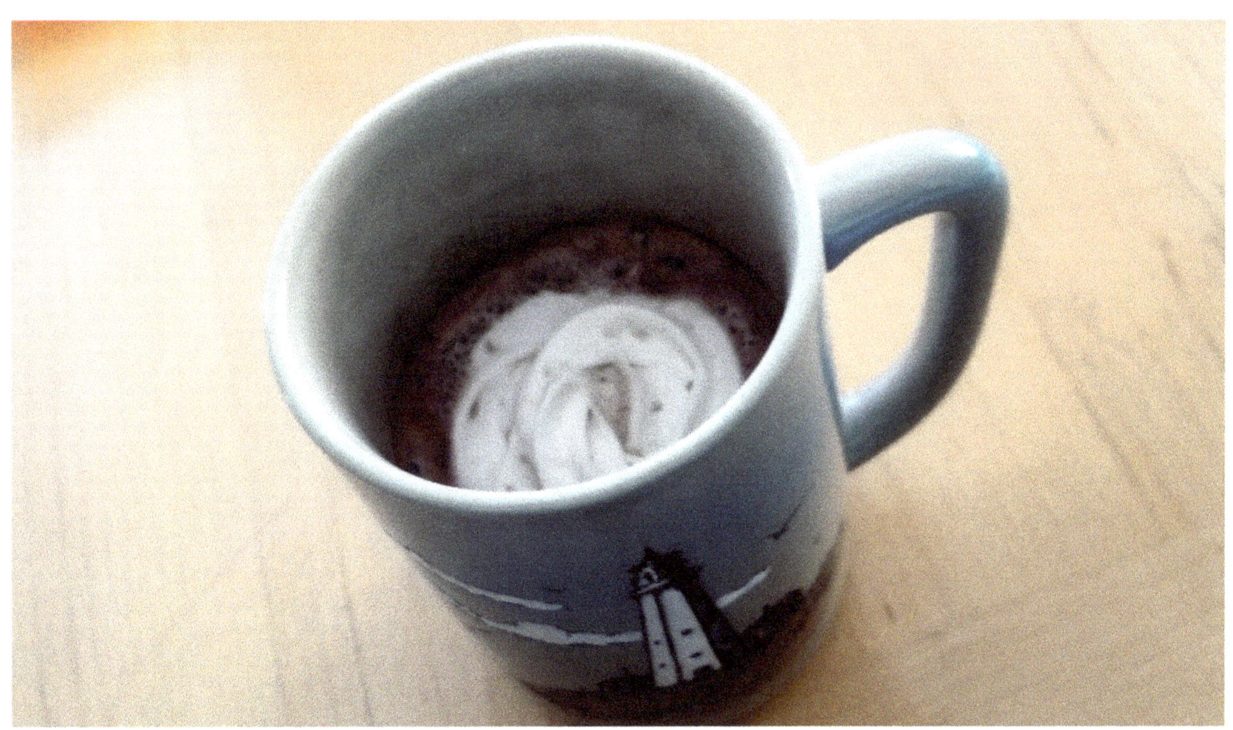

Memories of Mom

A lissome figure
bathed in lavender chiffon robe
and blush-hued feathery slippers,
shuffles towards break of day.
Soft tangerine glow peeks through window panes.

A tousle of auburn tresses
fall within sight.
Gently, she tucks
a billowy strand
behind delicate ears.

The perfect amount of Folgers is
measured, then shaken in the metal basket.
Ambrosial fragrance teases nostrils.
She grins with delight
as if savoring
the smell of earth after a light rain.

Bacon sizzles in the iron skillet.
Eggshells crack against ceramic.
Cackle, soon to be muddled beyond
recognition.

A saffron-hued percolator releases steam.
The bewitching aroma lures him from the serenity
of slumber.

Butterfly kisses alight on the nape of her neck,
as he lingers in her effervescence.

Every morning they do the dance.
Every morning they take the chance, at love.

Peering over cat-eye bifocals,
she raises a cuppa joe to pouty lips.

Bathing crisp bacon in fluid sunshine,
he pauses, admiring her zygomatics.
Riffling papers searching
the comic section
for Blondie and Dagwood...

Every morning they do the dance.
Every morning,
They take the chance,
At love.

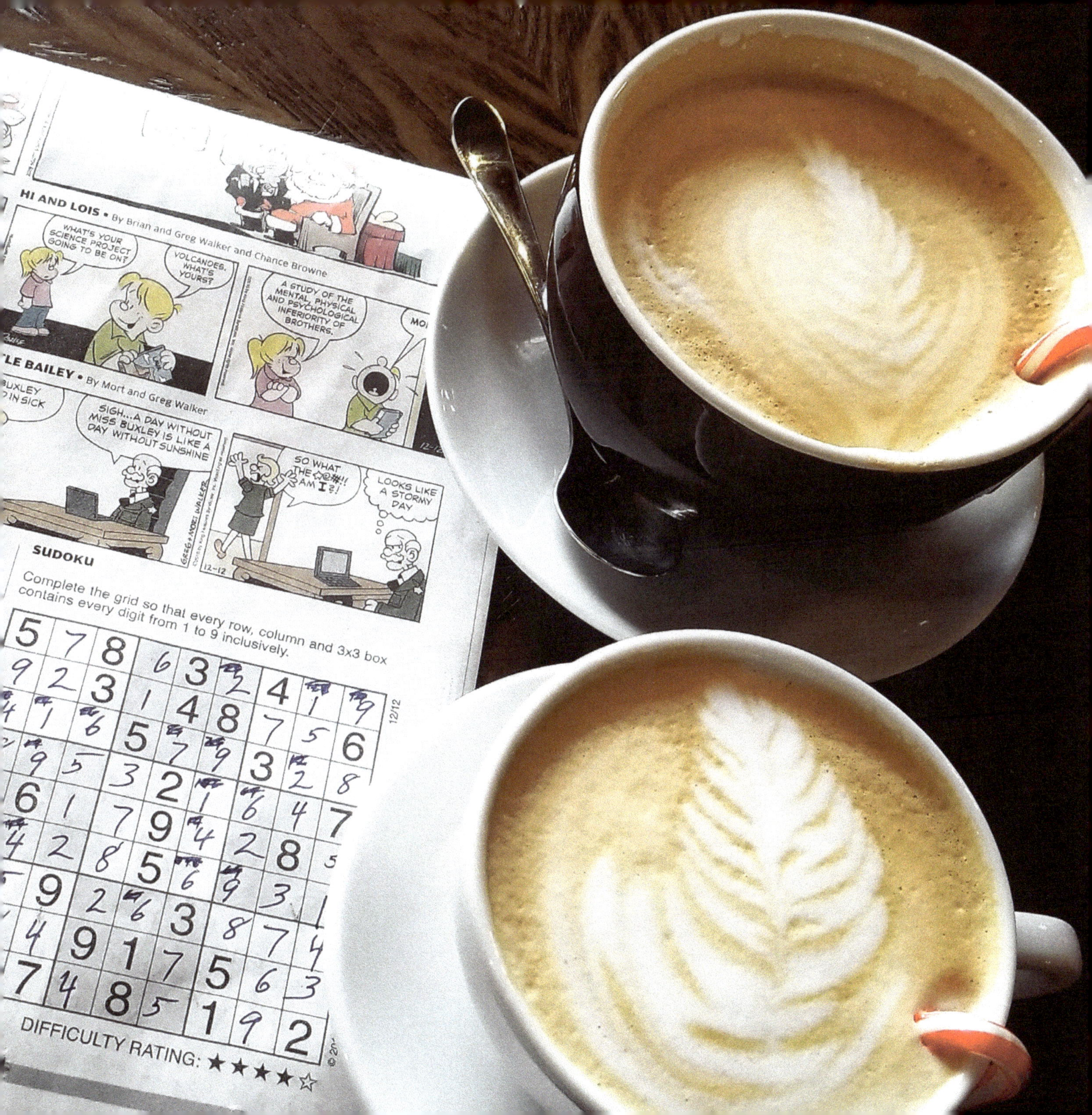
HI AND LOIS • By Brian and Greg Walker and Chance Browne
WHAT'S YOUR SCIENCE PROJECT GOING TO BE ON?
VOLCANOES. WHAT'S YOURS?
A STUDY OF THE MENTAL, PHYSICAL AND PSYCHOLOGICAL INFERIORITY OF BROTHERS.
TLE BAILEY • By Mort and Greg Walker
SIGH...A DAY WITHOUT MISS BUXLEY IS LIKE A DAY WITHOUT SUNSHINE
SO WHAT THE @#!! AM I?!
LOOKS LIKE A STORMY DAY
SUDOKU
Complete the grid so that every row, column and 3x3 box contains every digit from 1 to 9 inclusively.
12/12
DIFFICULTY RATING: ★★★★☆

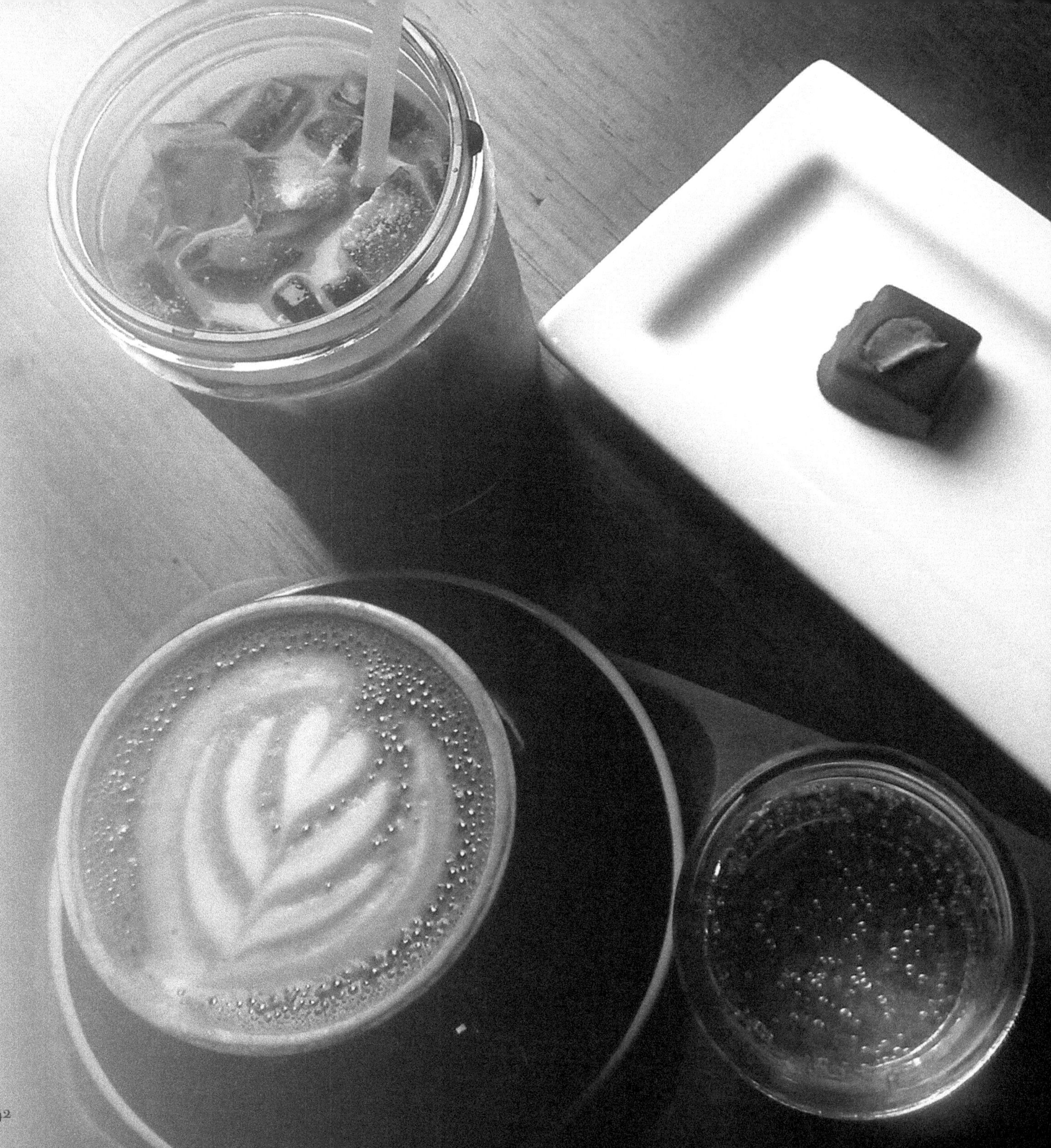

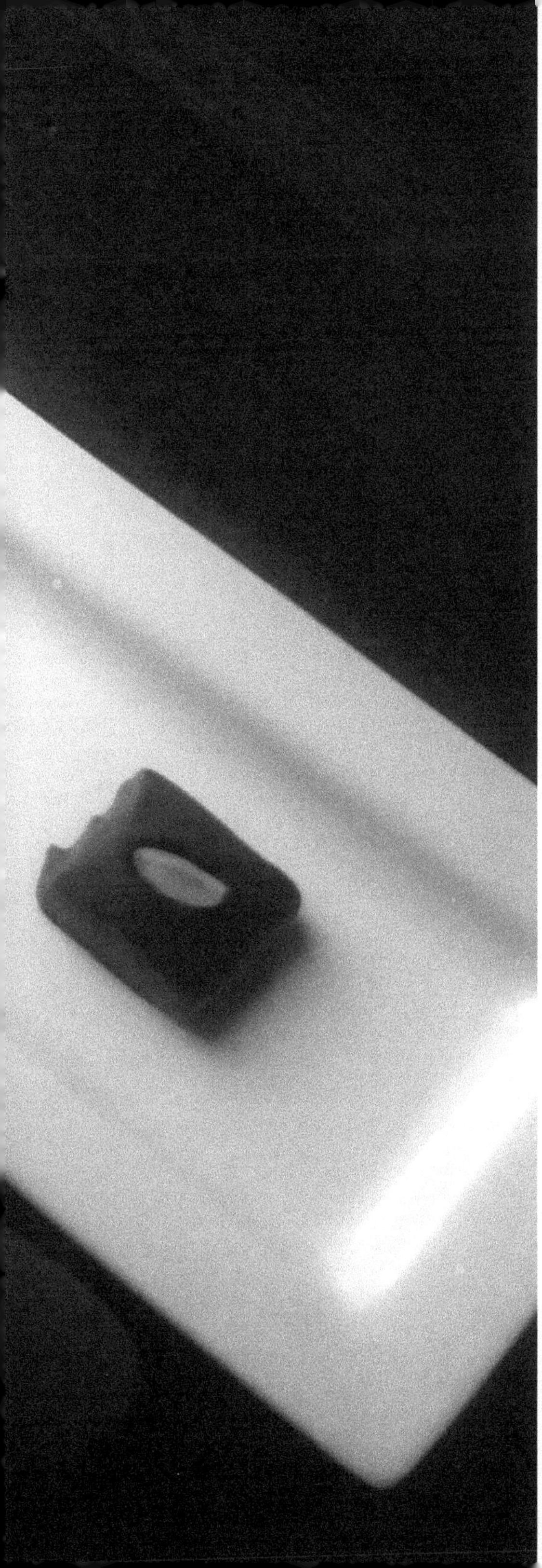

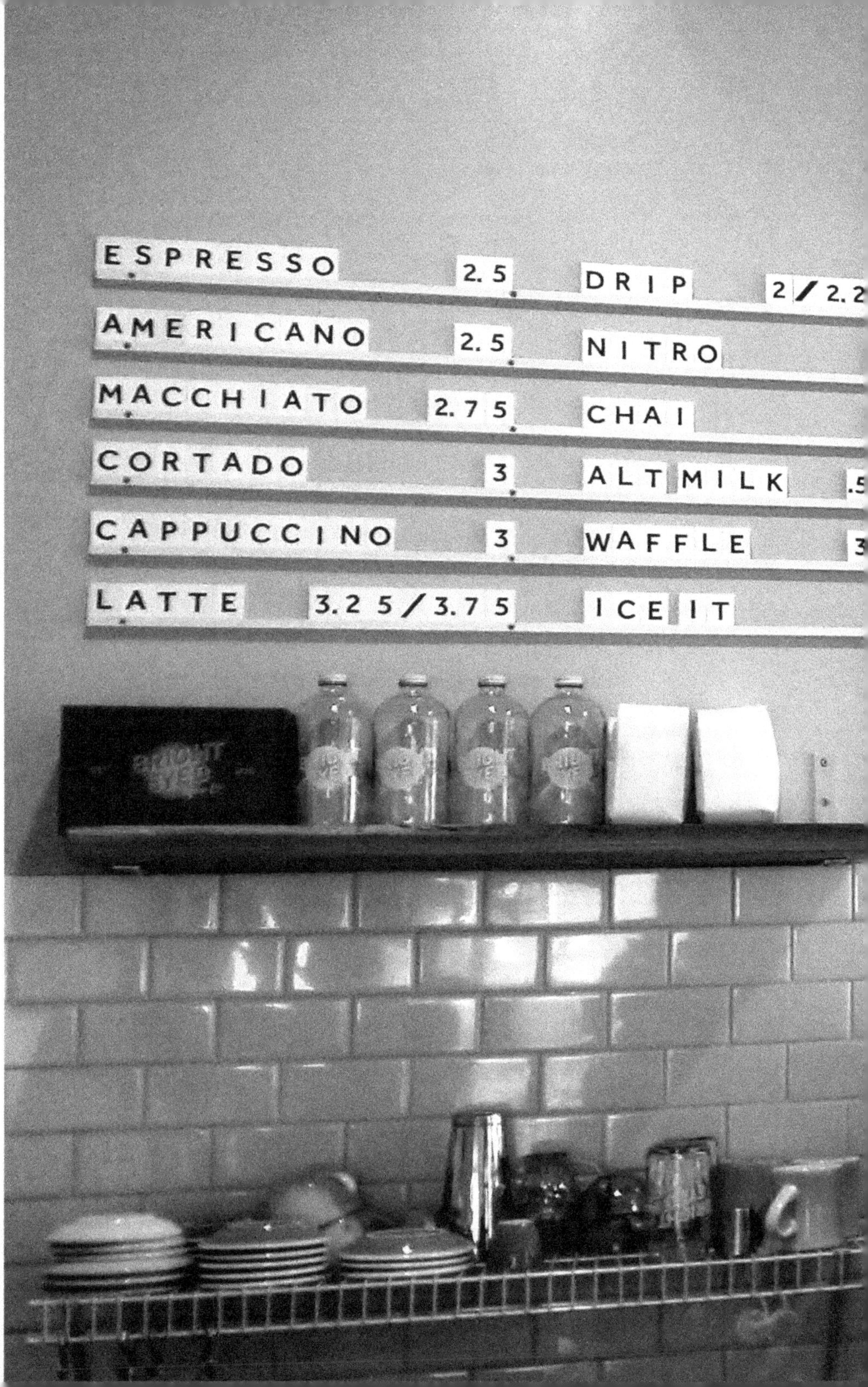

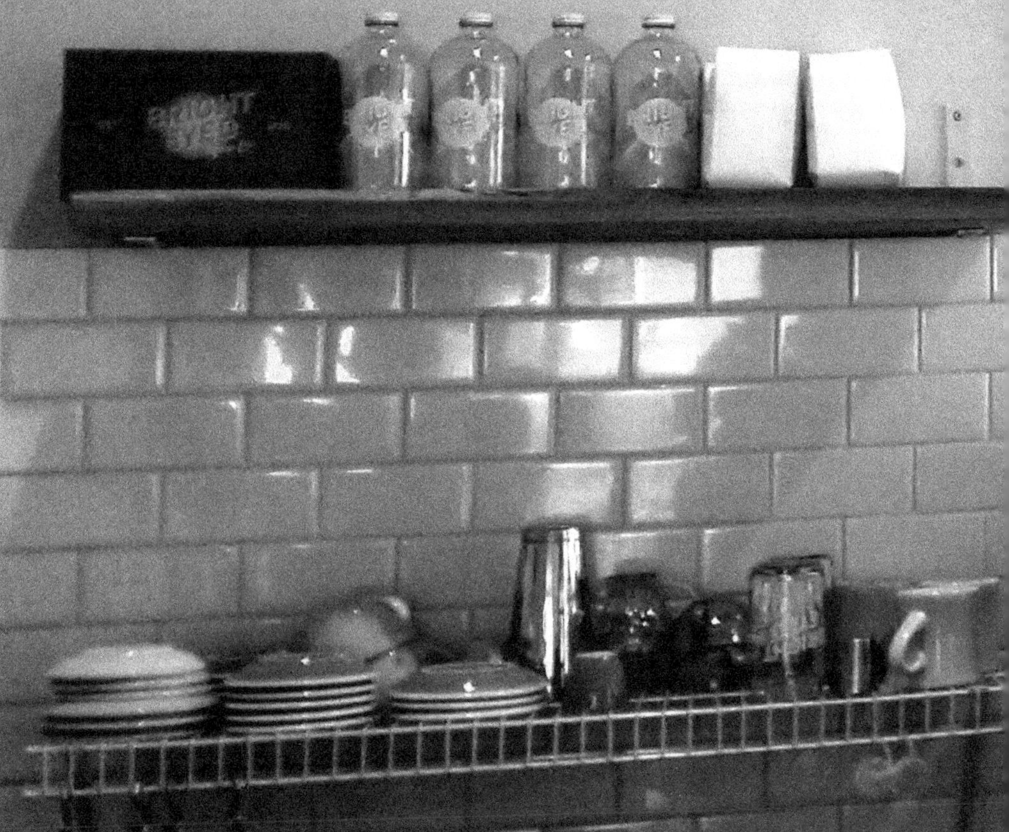

ESPRESSO 2.5
DRIP 2/2.2
AMERICANO 2.5
NITRO
MACCHIATO 2.75
CHAI
CORTADO 3
ALT MILK .5
CAPPUCCINO 3
WAFFLE 3
LATTE 3.25/3.75
ICE IT

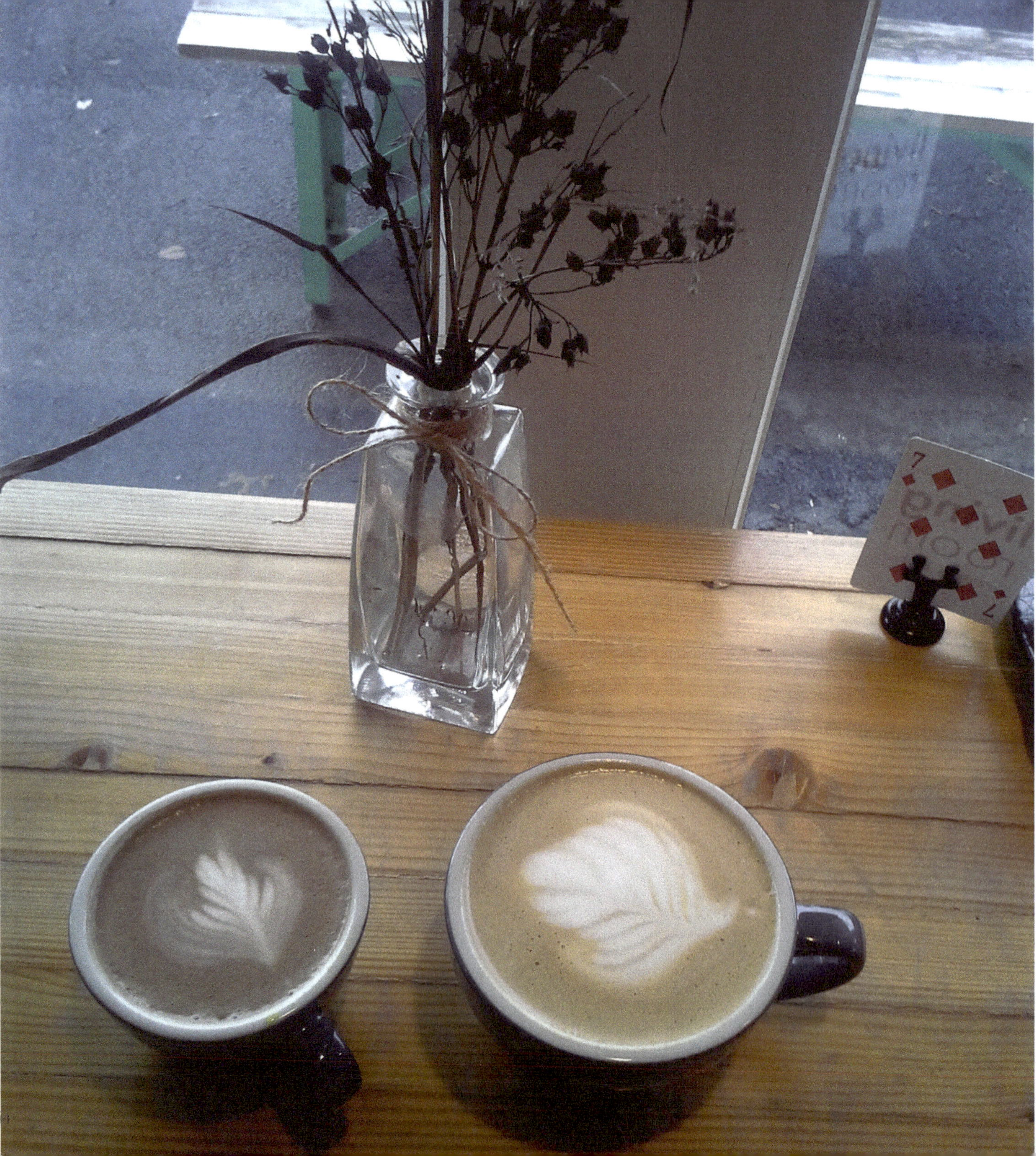

Coffee Date

Stealing glances…

Those ice-blue
eyes.

You lift
the cup
to pouty
full
lips.
Slow,
deliberate
sips.

Caramel foam compliments
your ginger
moustache.

Getting
to know you.

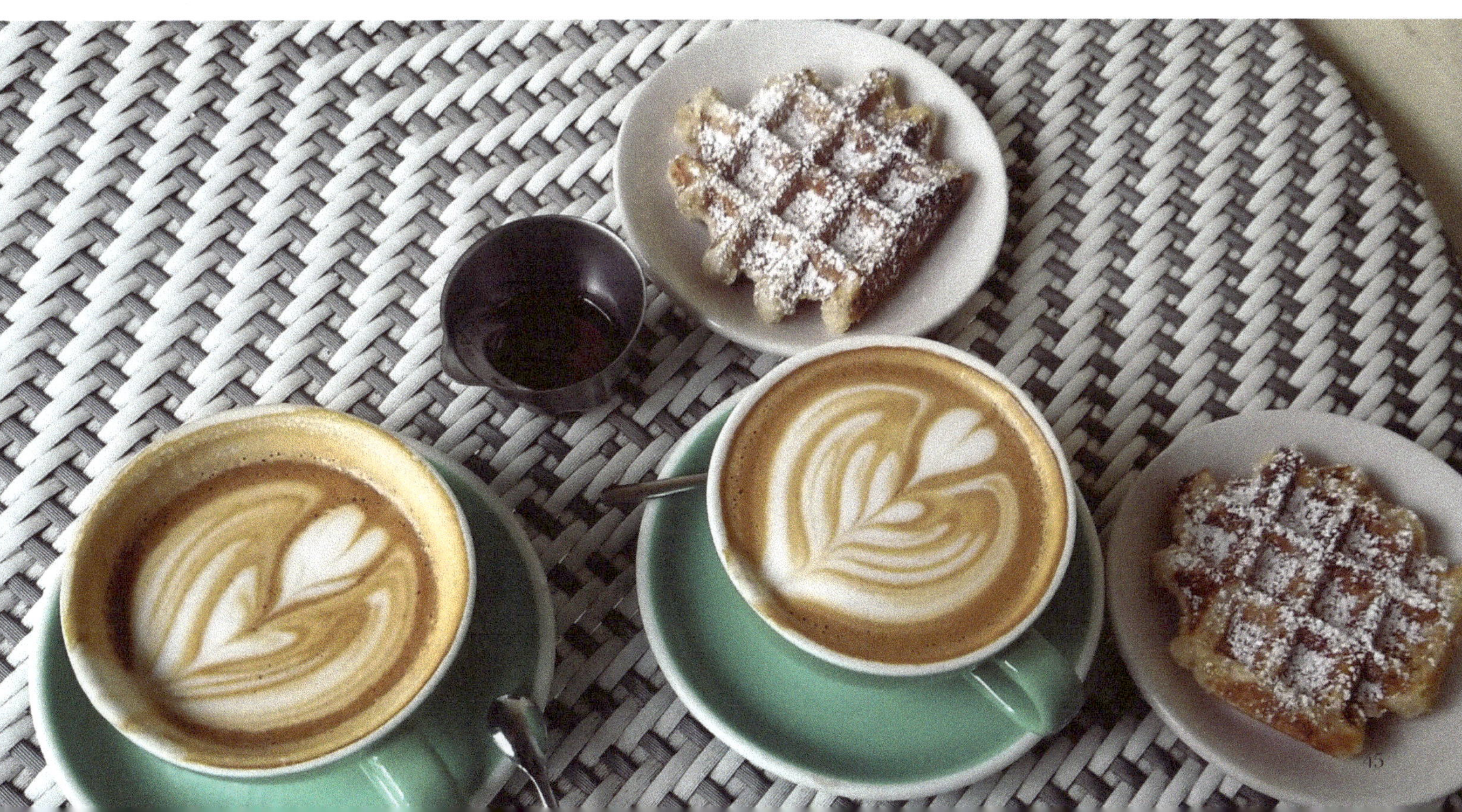

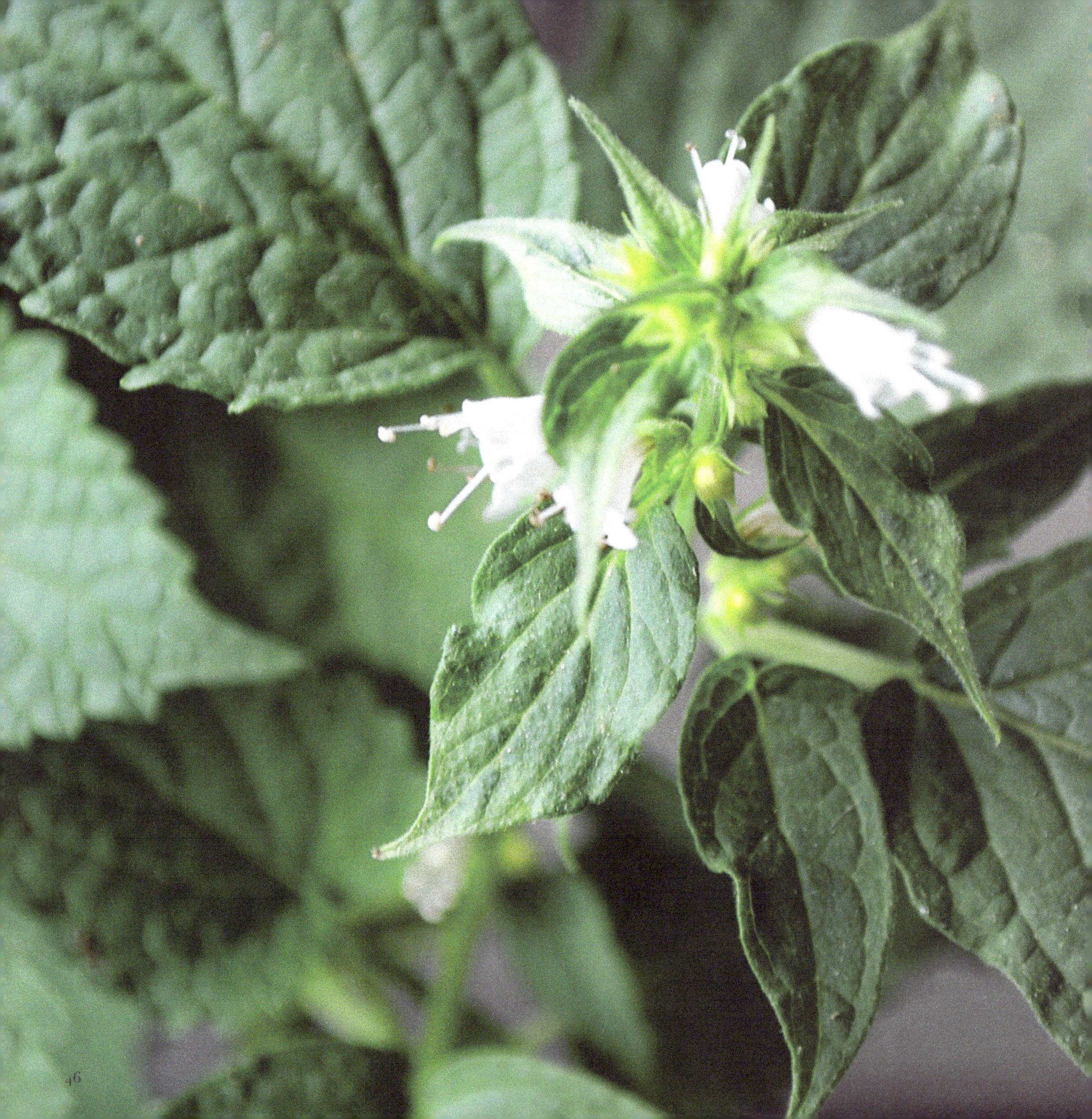

Kiss

hyssop nectar to a goldfinch

the taste of licorice on his lips

Conversation

Misty August rain
embraces boundaries
of the covered porch.

A Rose of Sharon sheds blooms
atop a lush cover
of fern-hued grass,
as Pretty Dog slumbers
on the cool surface
of the portico.

Red Dog whining,
fixes a gaze
on two hound dogs
frolicking
across the way.

Lover hands me
a freshly brewed cappuccino
in a tall ebony mug,
and garners a seat
on the faded Adirondack.

Willingly disposed
for stimulating
conversation . . .

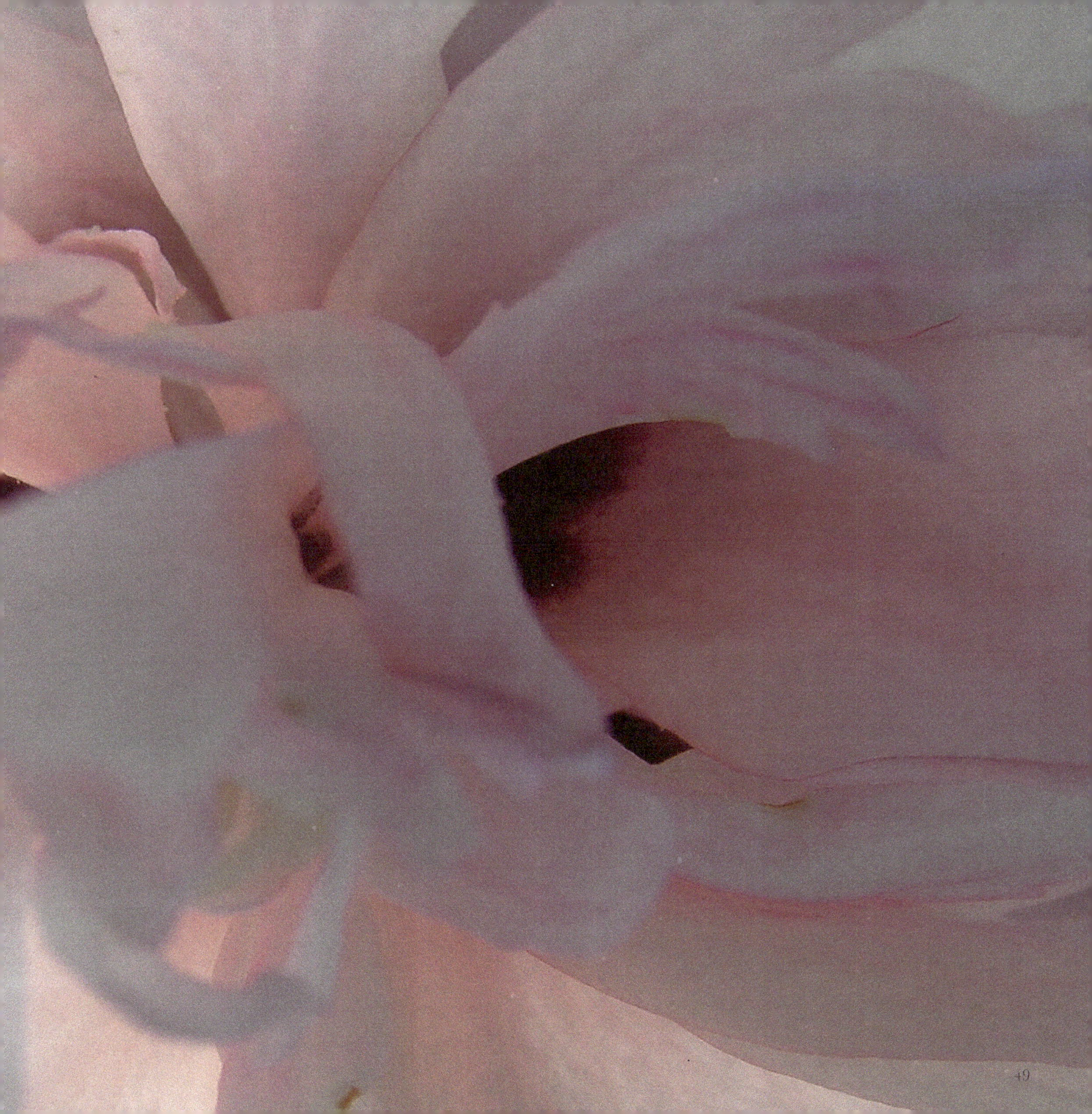

Smile

Affogato

Affogato!
How do I love thee?

I love you to the depths
of creamy vanilla
wholesomeness
and bitter
deliciousness!

Eager lips
crave your decadent
espresso crème –
cool, yet warm
to the touch.

Evanescent
is your full-bodied
shape enrobed in
layers of rich, tan
elixir...

Affogato!
Affogato!
I murmur your
sweet name.

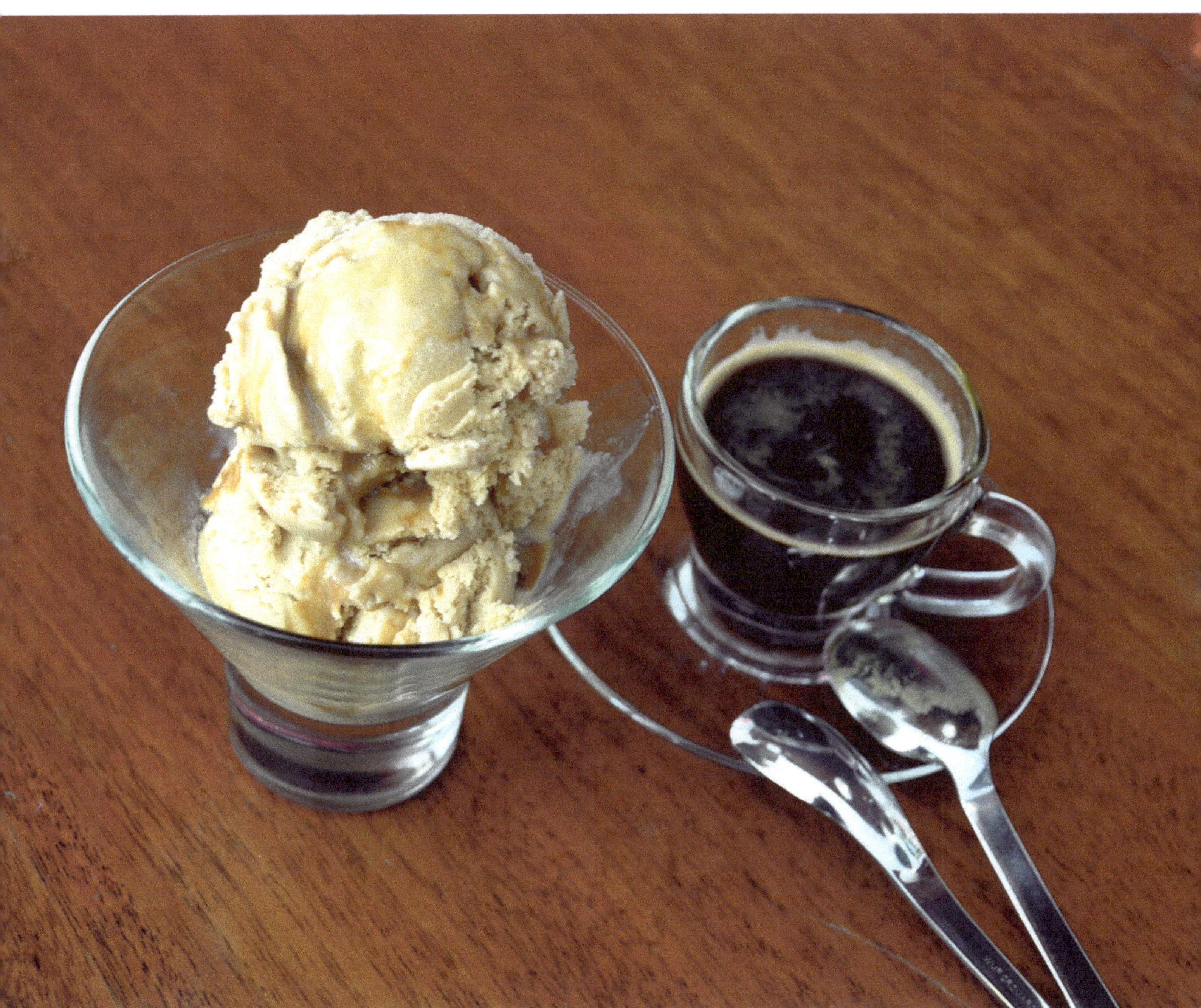

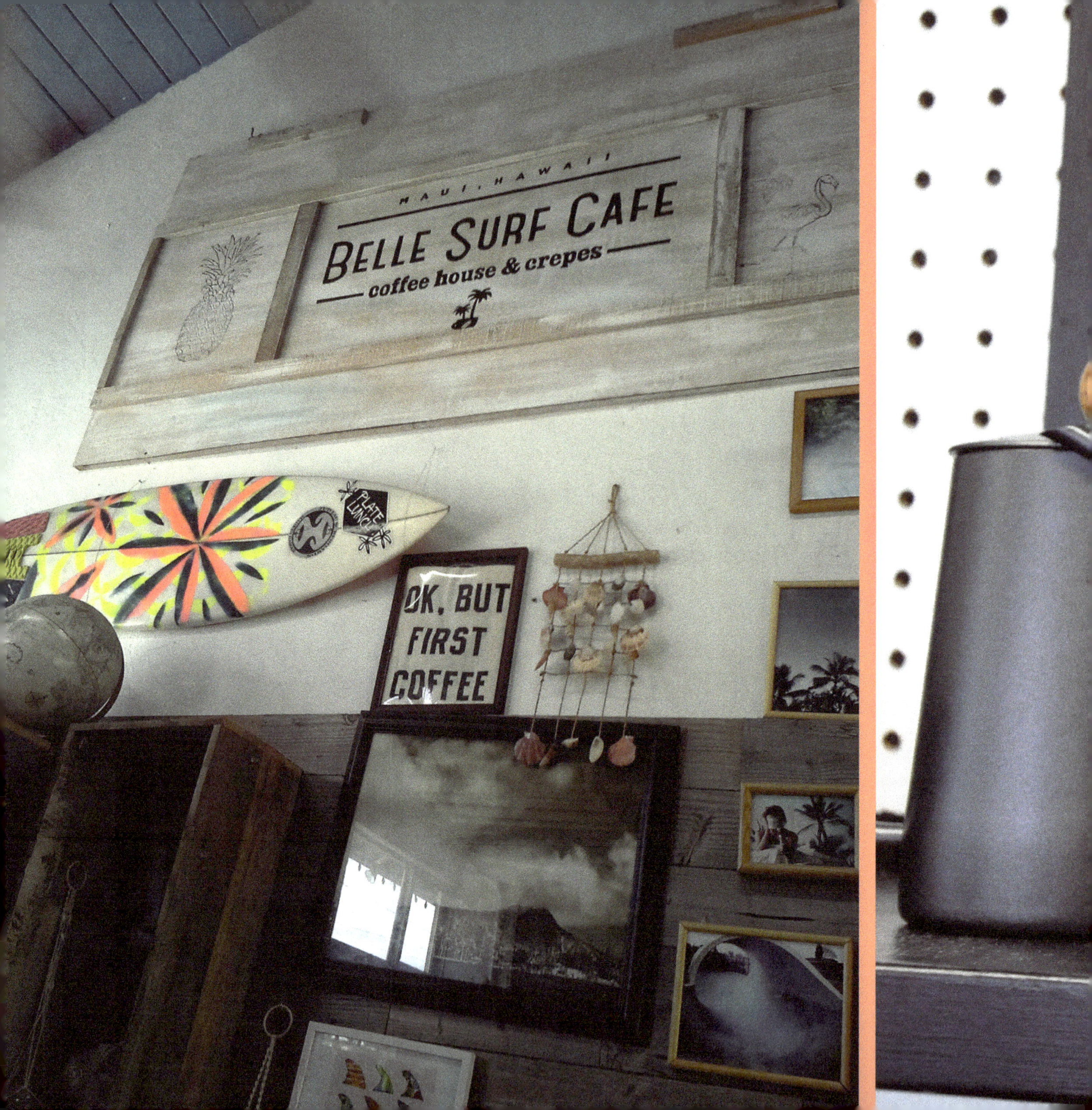
MAUI · HAWAII
BELLE SURF CAFE
coffee house & crepes
OK, BUT FIRST COFFEE

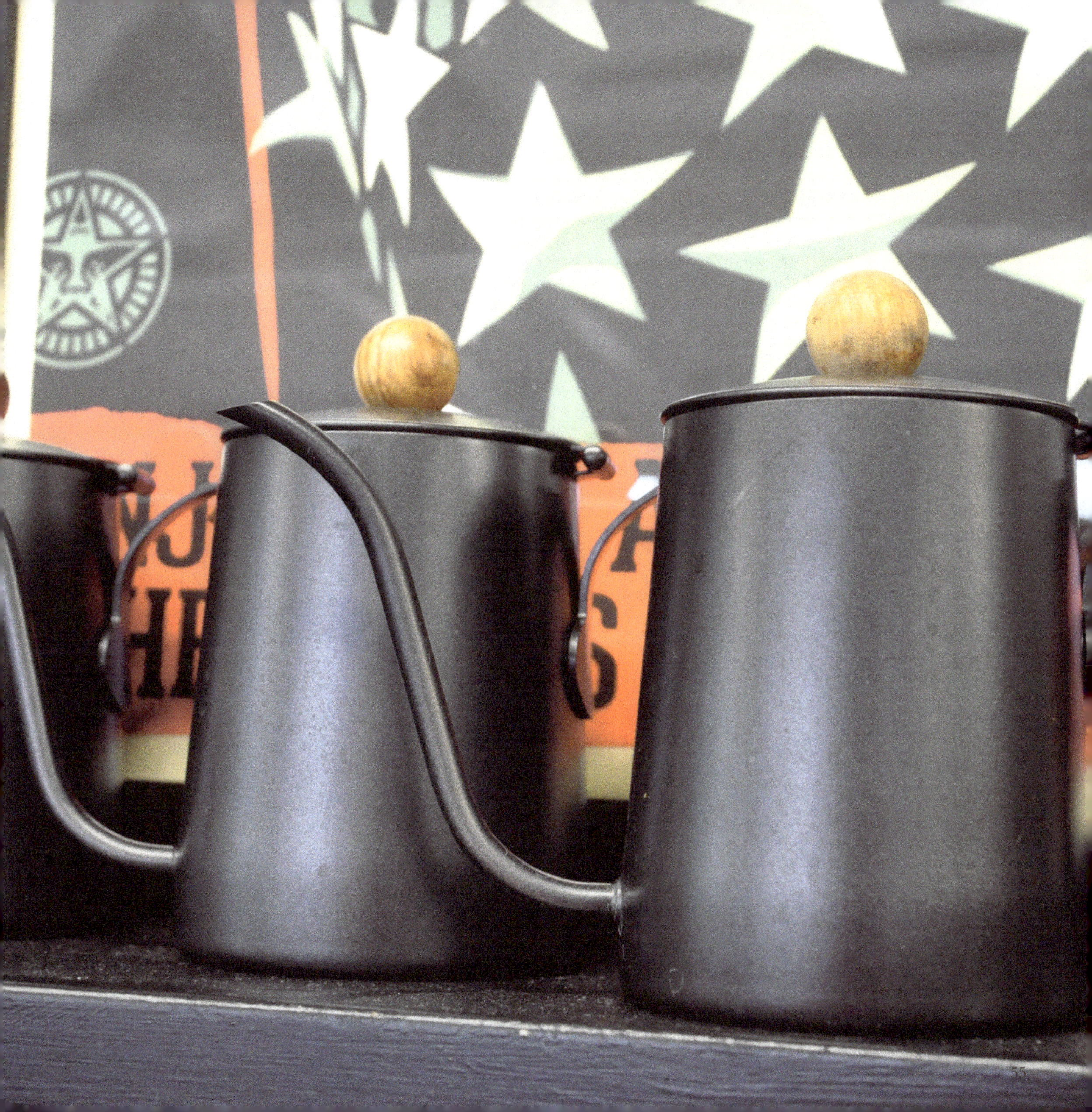

But First, Coffee

Docks to meander,
clothes to wash,
beaches to explore,
meals to prepare,
oceans to dive,
bills to pay,
boats to sail,
kitties to love,
goals to reach,
lakes to fish,
gardens to plant,
nature to admire,
dogs to walk,
sunsets to savor,
stories to be told,
tubs to soak in,
love to be made,
mountains to climb.

But First,
Coffee.

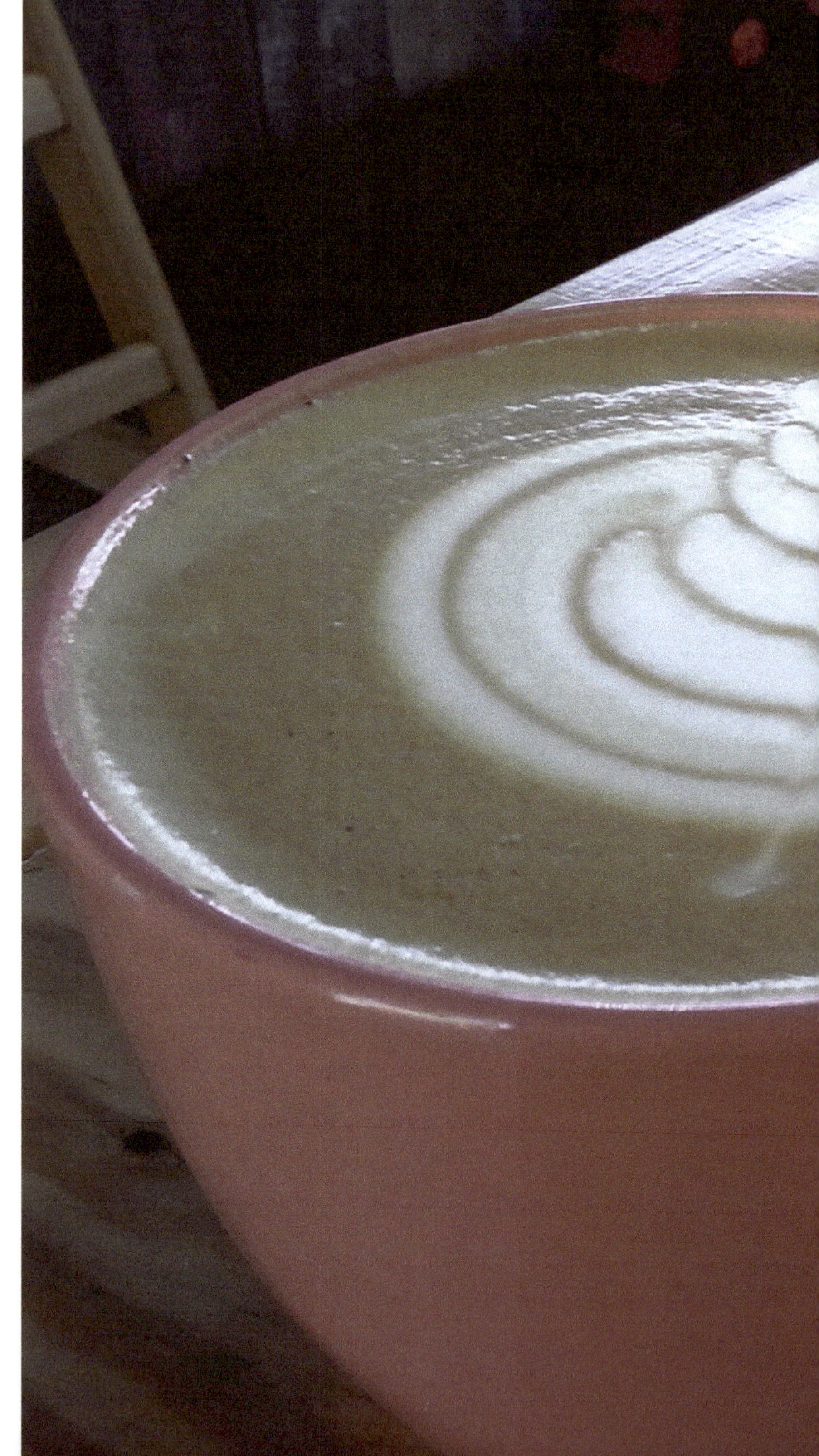

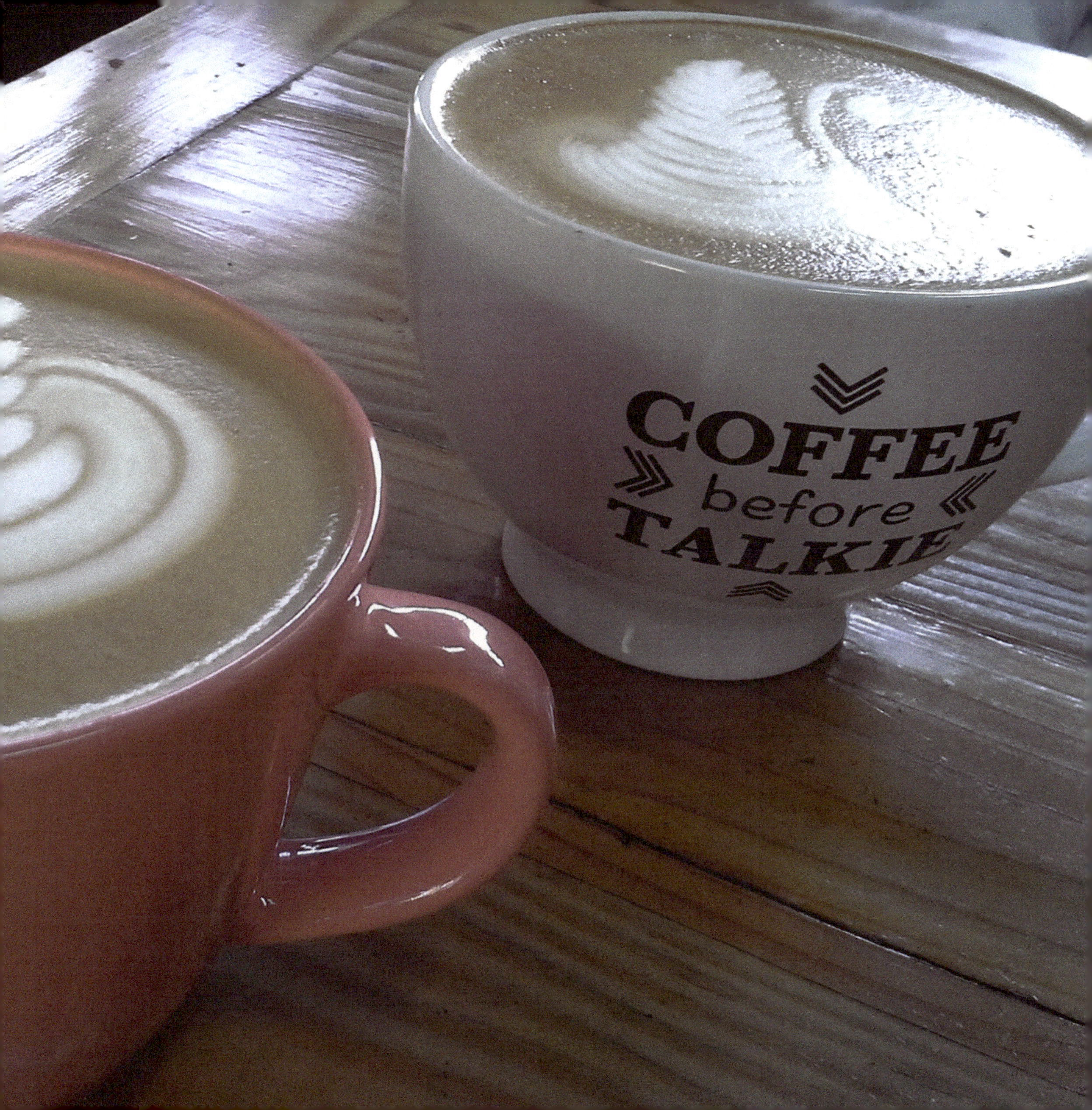
COFFEE
before
TALKIE

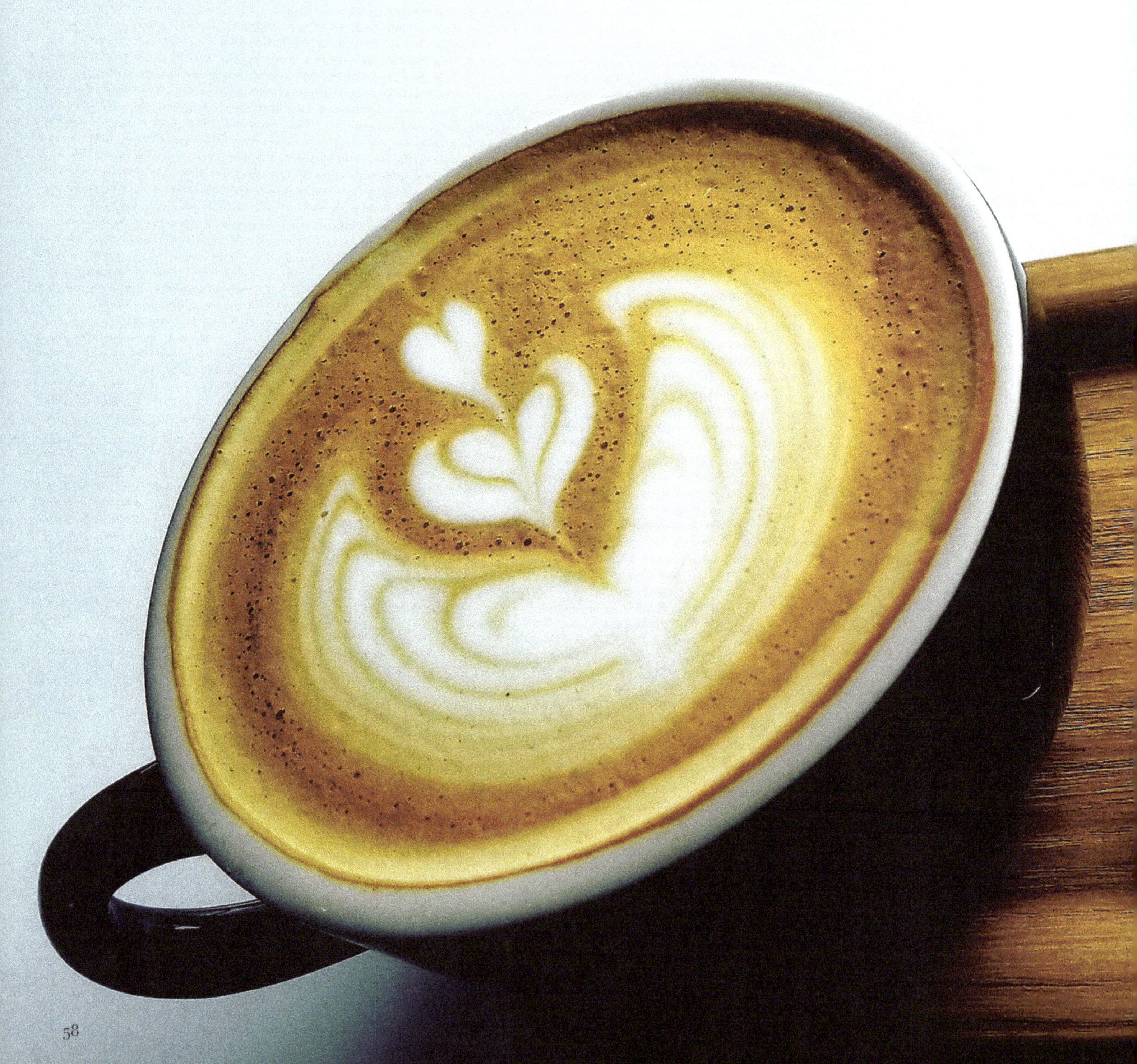

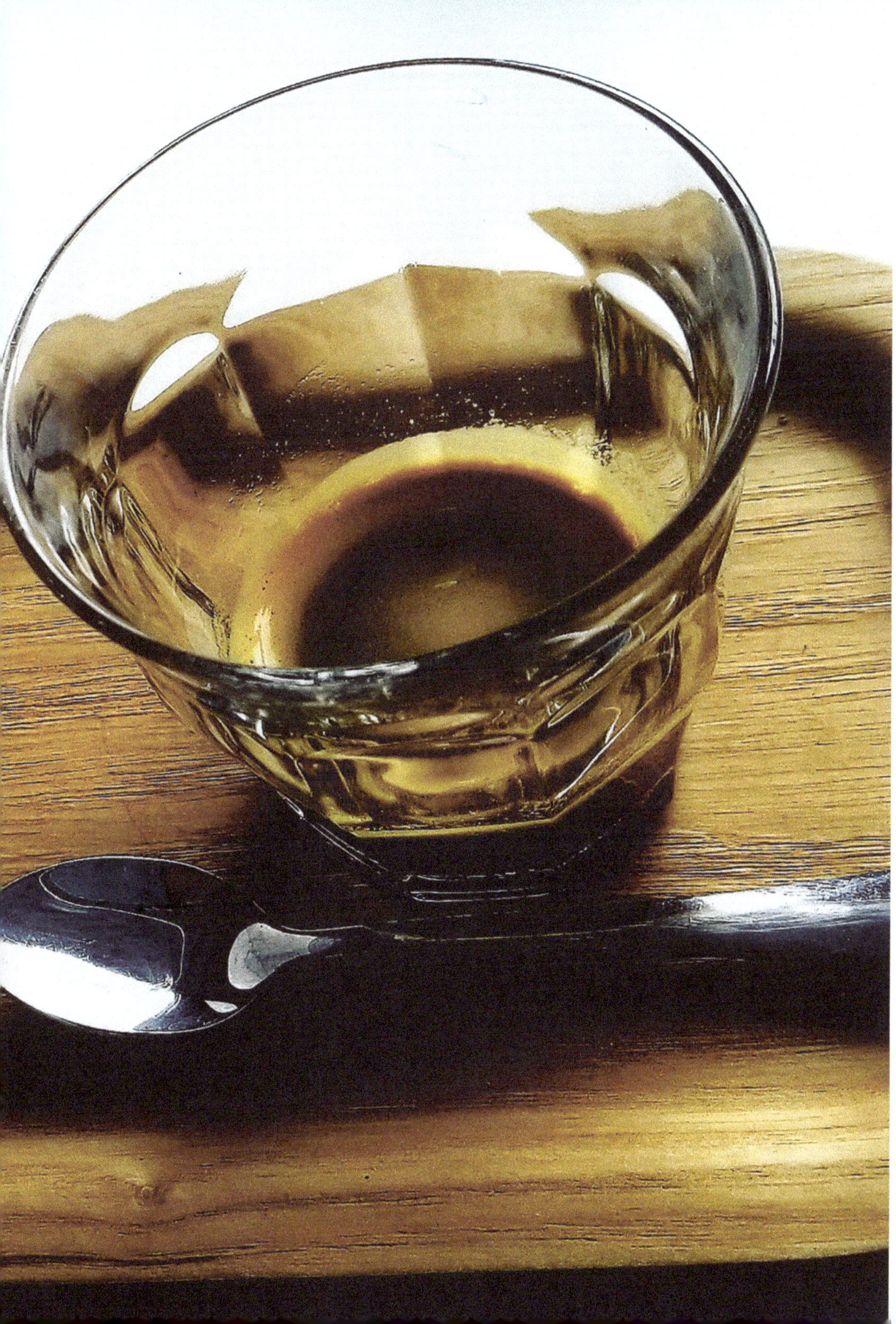

The Jitters

Can

Only

Function

Fully with

Extra shots of

Espresso

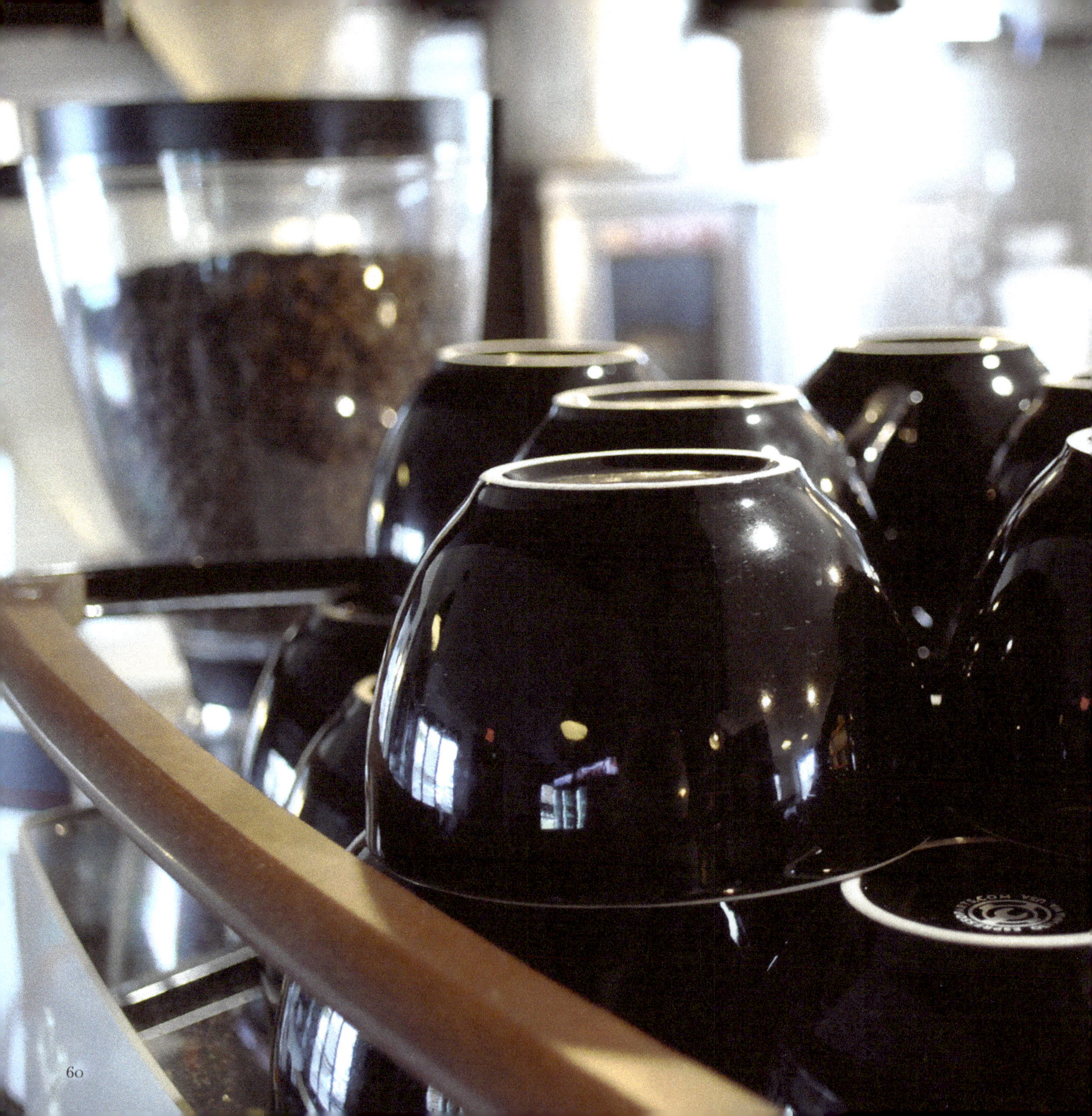

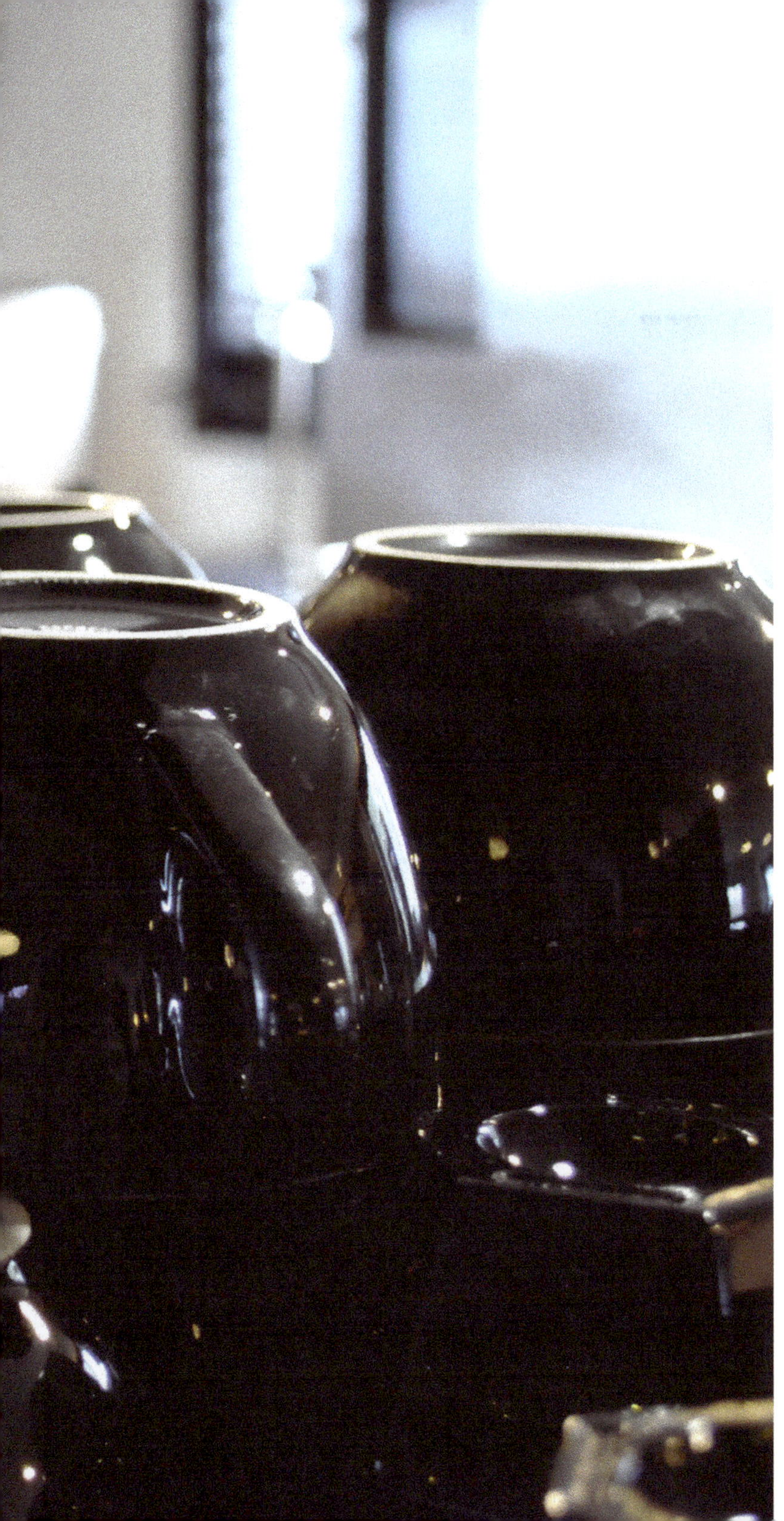

The Keur

You spew half truths
from your reservoir
that warns me
to fill you
up
lest your well
run dry.

You huff and you puff
and you drip
and spit
and spew from
your
tiny mouth
ubiquitous droplets,
saturating
my work in progress.

Brew me up some coffee,
you mean machine!

Mugs

Short mugs,
tall mugs,
thick mugs,
small mugs.

Mugs with red foxes,
or teal octopi,
mugs with swimming mermaids
that catch your eye.

Mugs from Mom
you received when Dad passed,
mugs from friends
you've known all your life.

Guitar playing cat
mugs stating,
"I'm in the band",
that fit like a dream
in the palm of your hand.

Mugs you take camping
or carry in your pack,
mugs painted on clay
for hubby with love.

Mugs collected from states
like Florida or Hawaii,
showcasing flamingos,
and the majestic sea.

Snippets of life,
these mugs are made for,
the good times, the bad times,
precious memories and more...

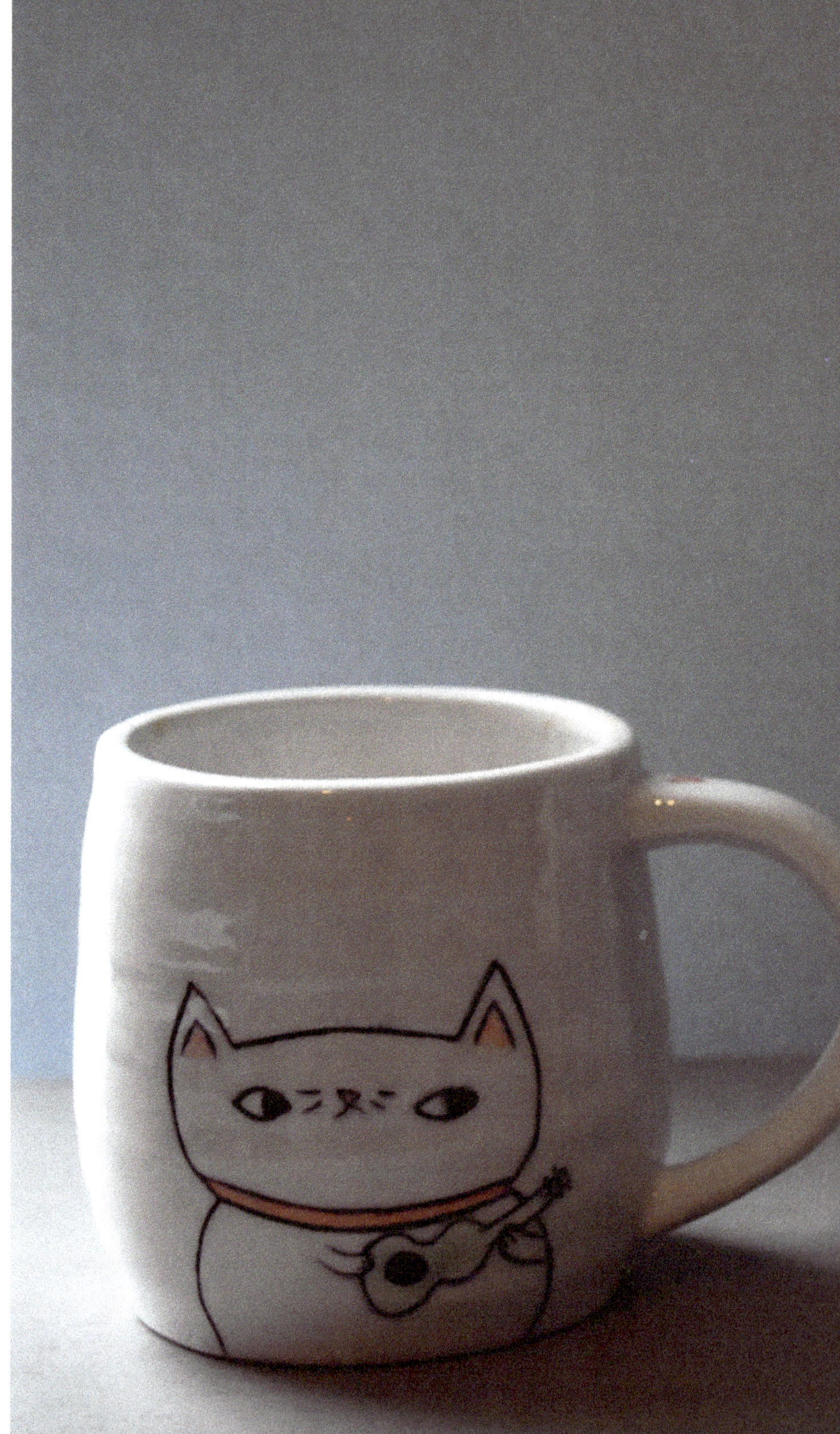

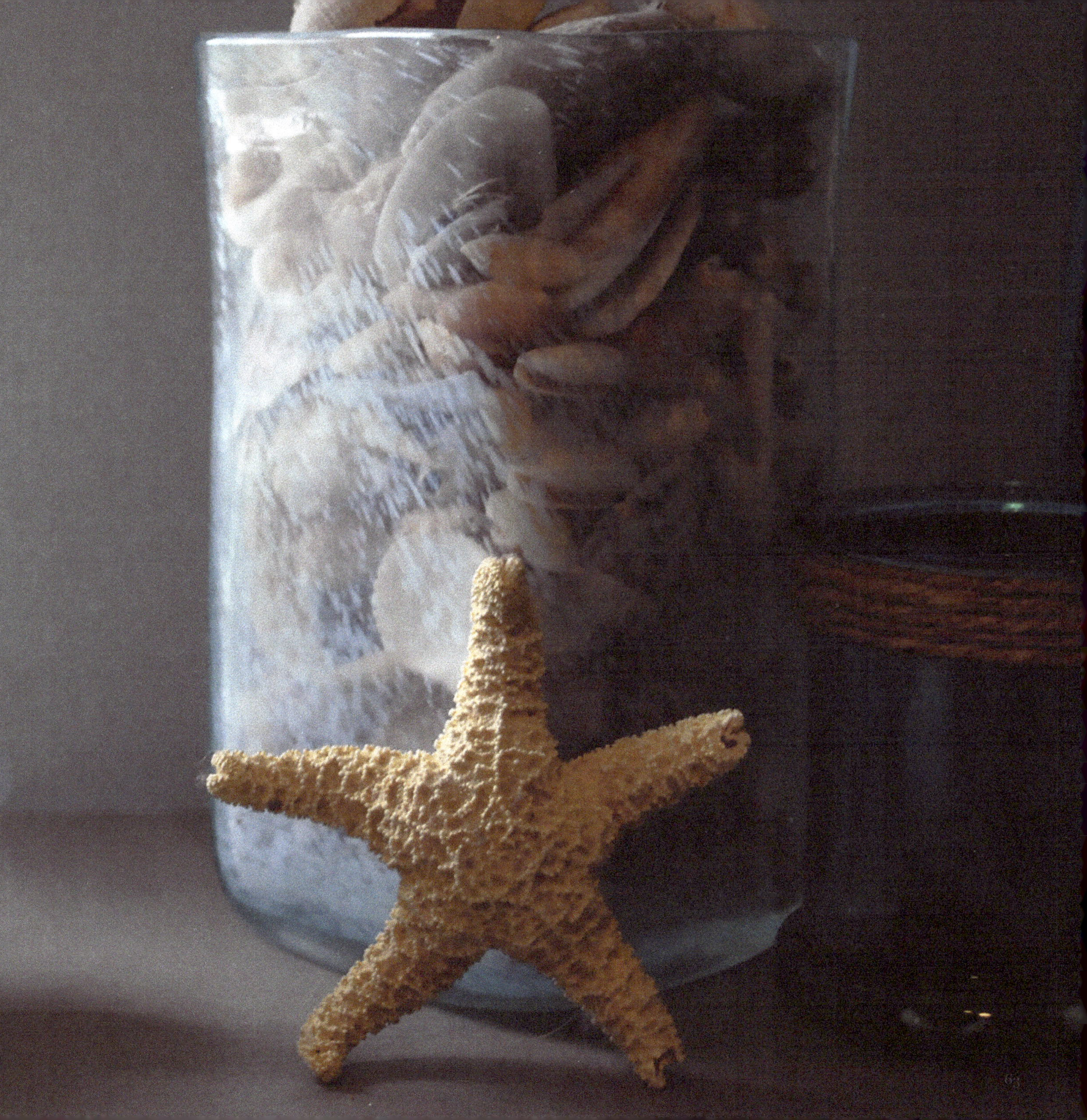

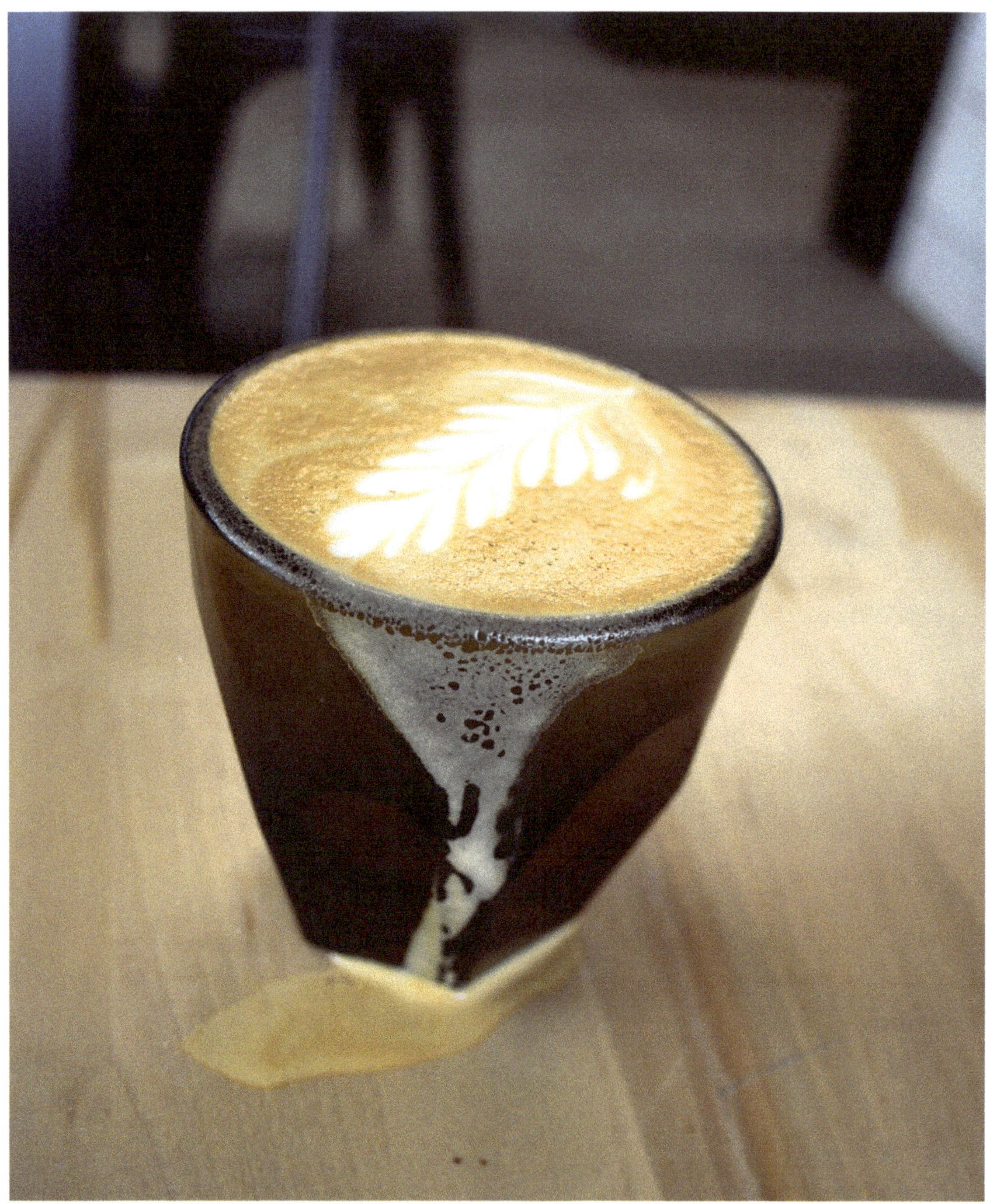

Don't Cry Over Spilled Coffee

How do you
like it?

Grande nonfat
iced
cappuccino ristretto
one pump mocha
extra foam.
Please?

The motion of lifting the cup
to eager lips
every so often
misses the mouth
on the first try.

In such maladroit
instances,
it's okay to substitute
sidewalk art
for beverage sipping.

Life

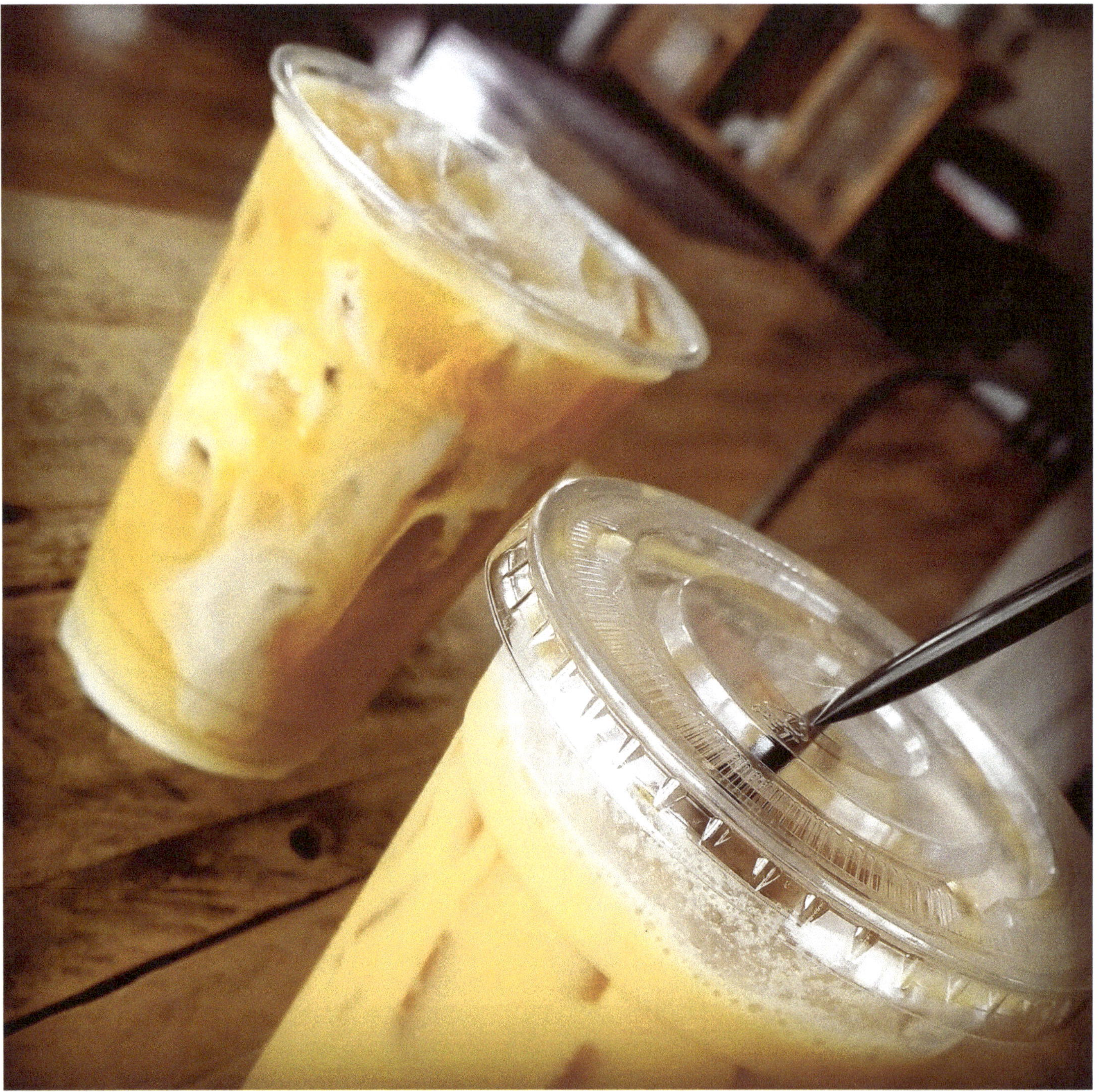

Latte with Friends

Warm wood of café tables
invite as friends gather
for fellowship
and conversation.

There's something to be said
about the
aroma of a vanilla latte,
chatter of nearby patrons...
an espresso machine's
agreeable noise,
encouraging transparency.

Listen closely to the chatter...
you'll hear stories
of financial loss,
long walks on the shore,
love rekindled,
the birth of a granddaughter,
snuggles with Fido.

Long-time friends
laugh,
embrace
imperfection, purpose,
nature,
each other.

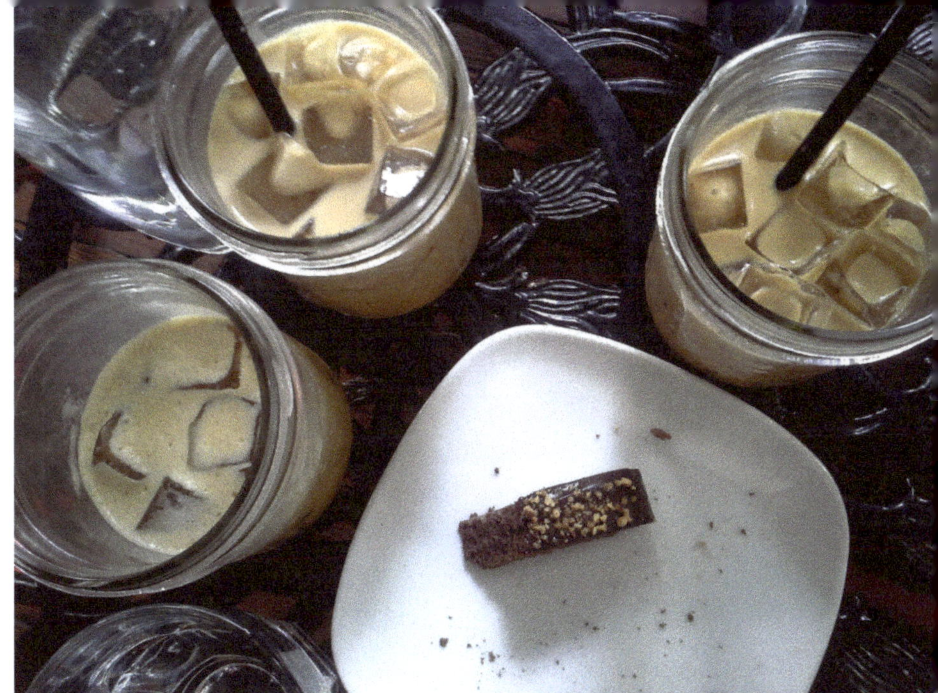

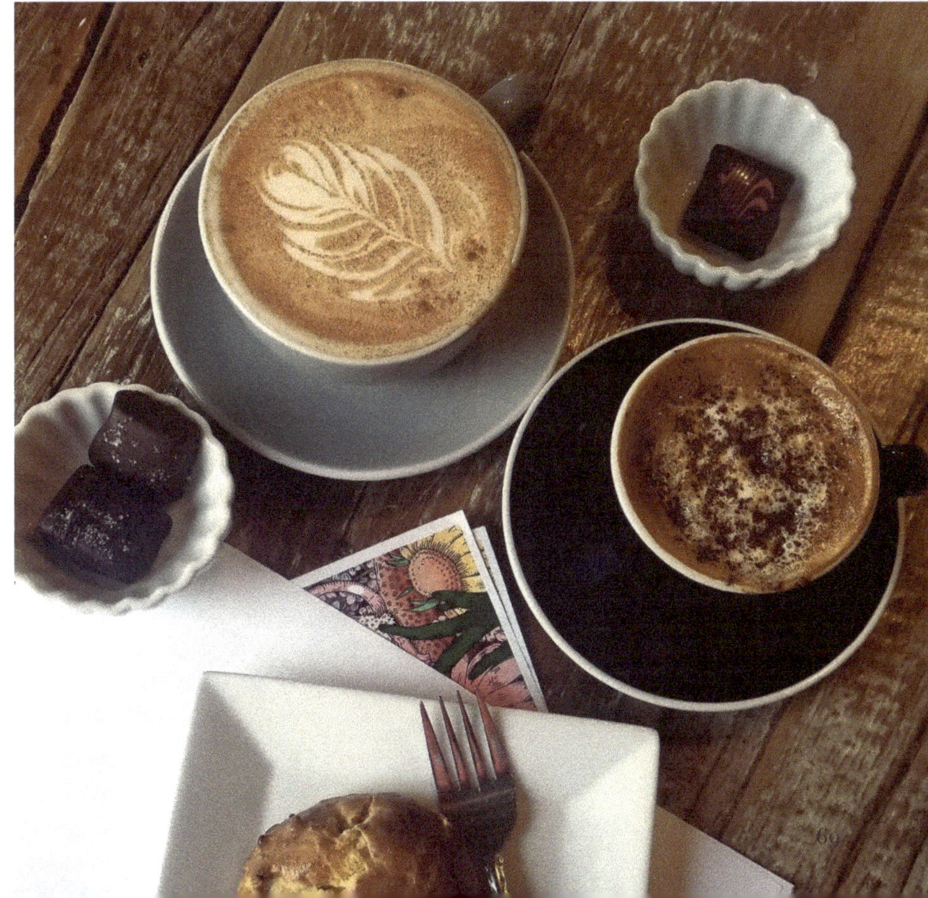

Sunday Drive

Driving on rutted back roads,
passing rushing creeks,
exploring abandoned harbors,
rusty old red
house boats.
No trespassing signs.
Flooded paths to nowhere.
Homes awash in faded memories . . .

Mysteries never solved.
Great herons and snow geese conceal
fiery secrets hidden
in marsh flats.

Driving on back roads
sipping cappuccinos,
another Sunday afternoon . . .

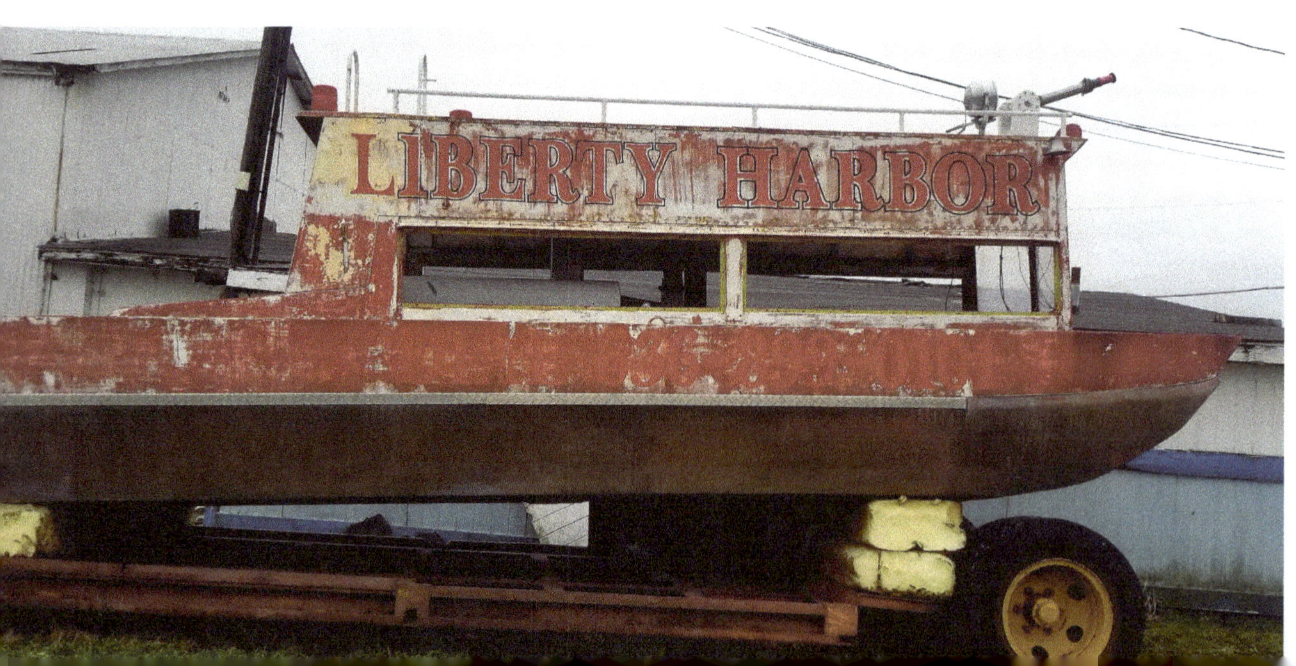

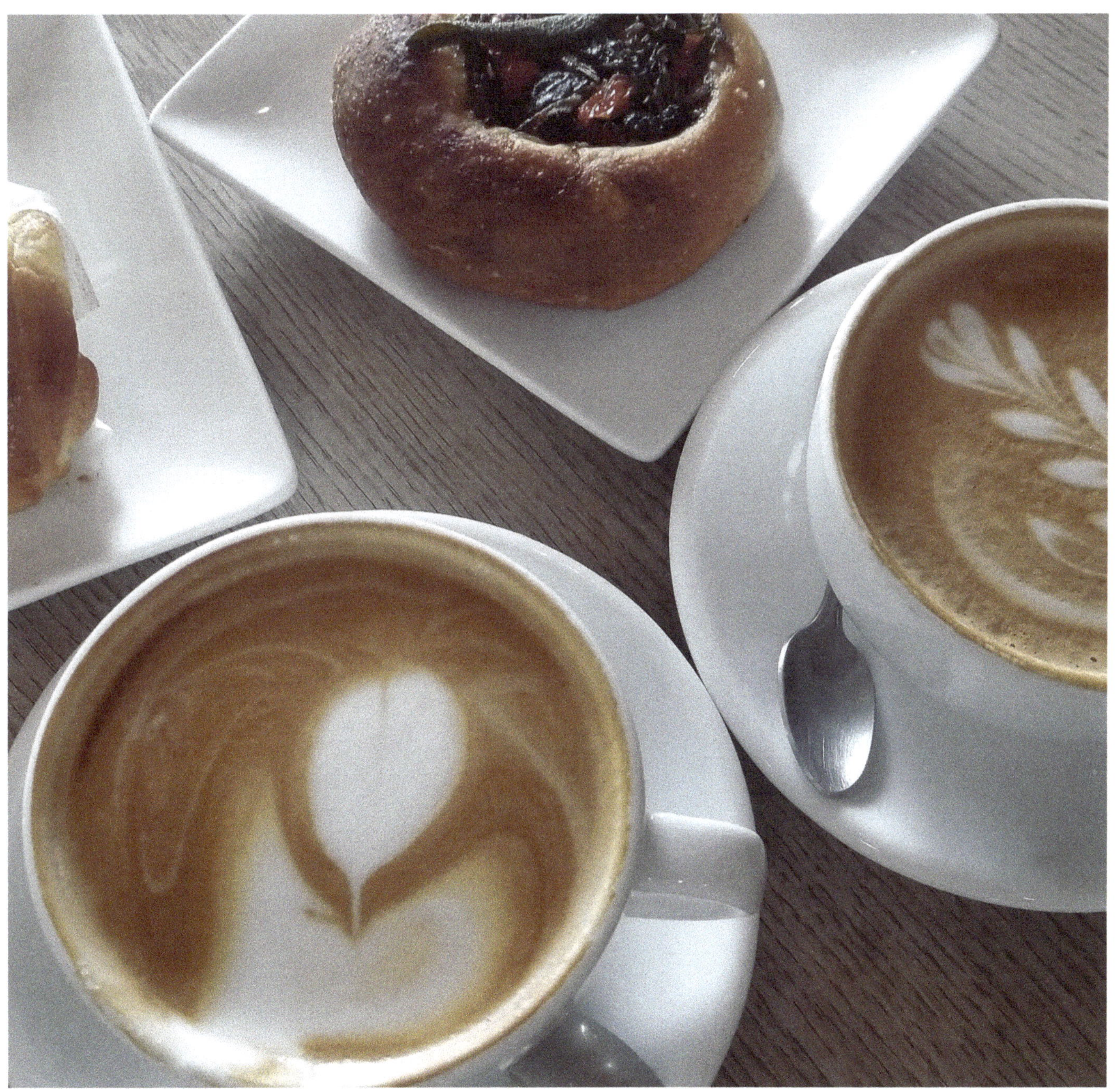

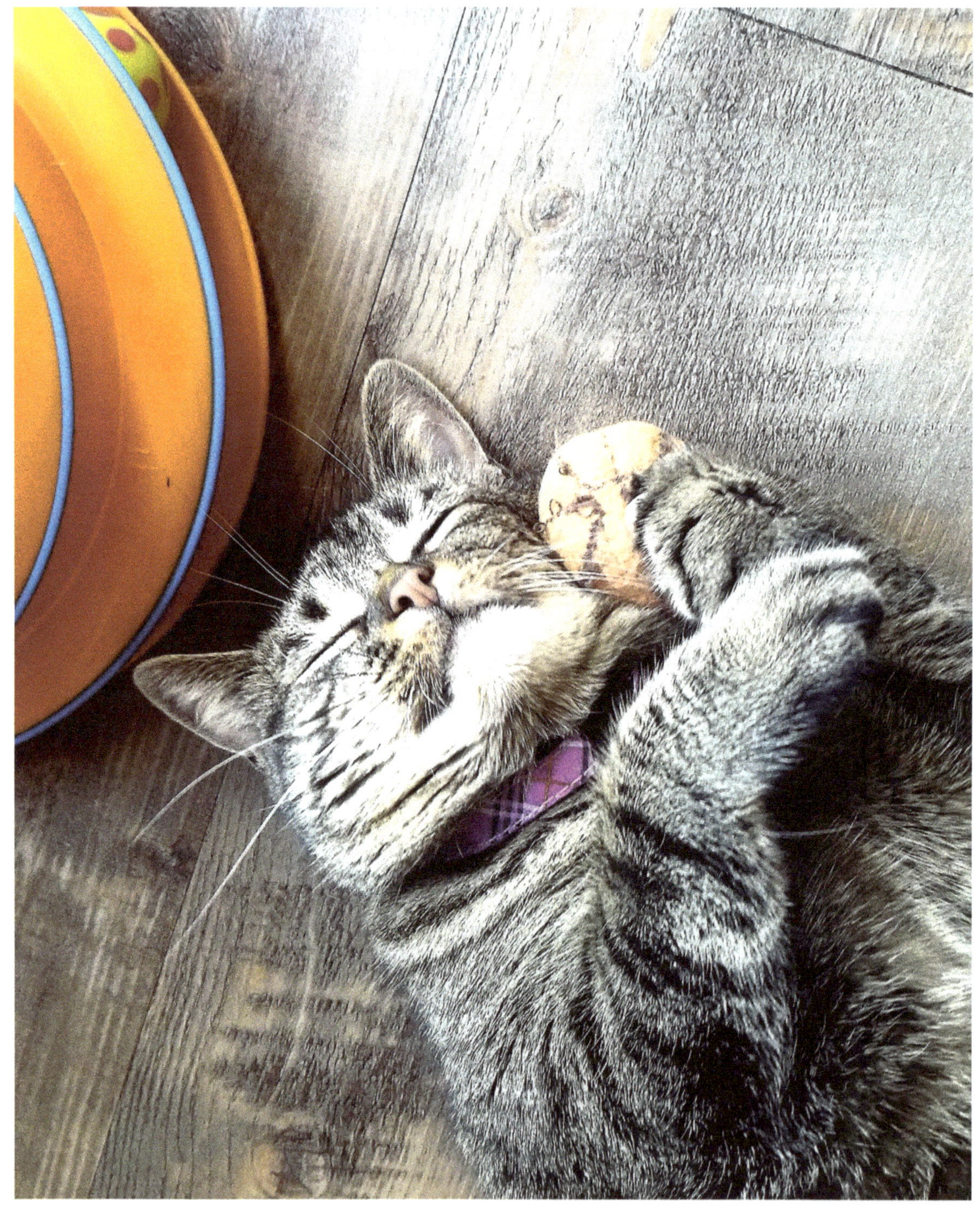

Coffee with Cats

I plop a dollop of whipped cream on my locally roasted coffee.
The ritual of table-sitting
begins.

Properly perched,
you can't help but notice
Batman ears, maize-grey eyes, and
perfectly pursed lips studying
dark eyed juncos, Carolina chickadees, and song sparrows foraging
seed
scattered about the wooden deck.

Lifting her box-like snout upward,
she sniffs,
then saunters across the table
to analyze the roast of the day
by dipping whiskers
into the fray,
not once, but twice.

Purring, she leaves scent on notebooks, knuckles, memo holders.
Prancing on papers, nudging me,
showing
beautiful 'toe beans',
purring, attentively observing
my composition,
sniffing coffee.

continued…

She stretches into downward facing dog,
and settles in, brushing my forearm,
allowing affection.
Coat like
gossamer on a black widow's web.

Pursed lips, sweet kisses, and nudges are more
than I can ask.
She showers me with a revered kind of
'kitty lovin'.

A cardinal lilting on the rails catches her eye,
as a glint of sunlight wraps a blanket of
warmth
around a dense tortoiseshell coat.

She's off again to dream her dreams of wanderlust
that fill her quite
exquisiteness.

Coffee with cats.

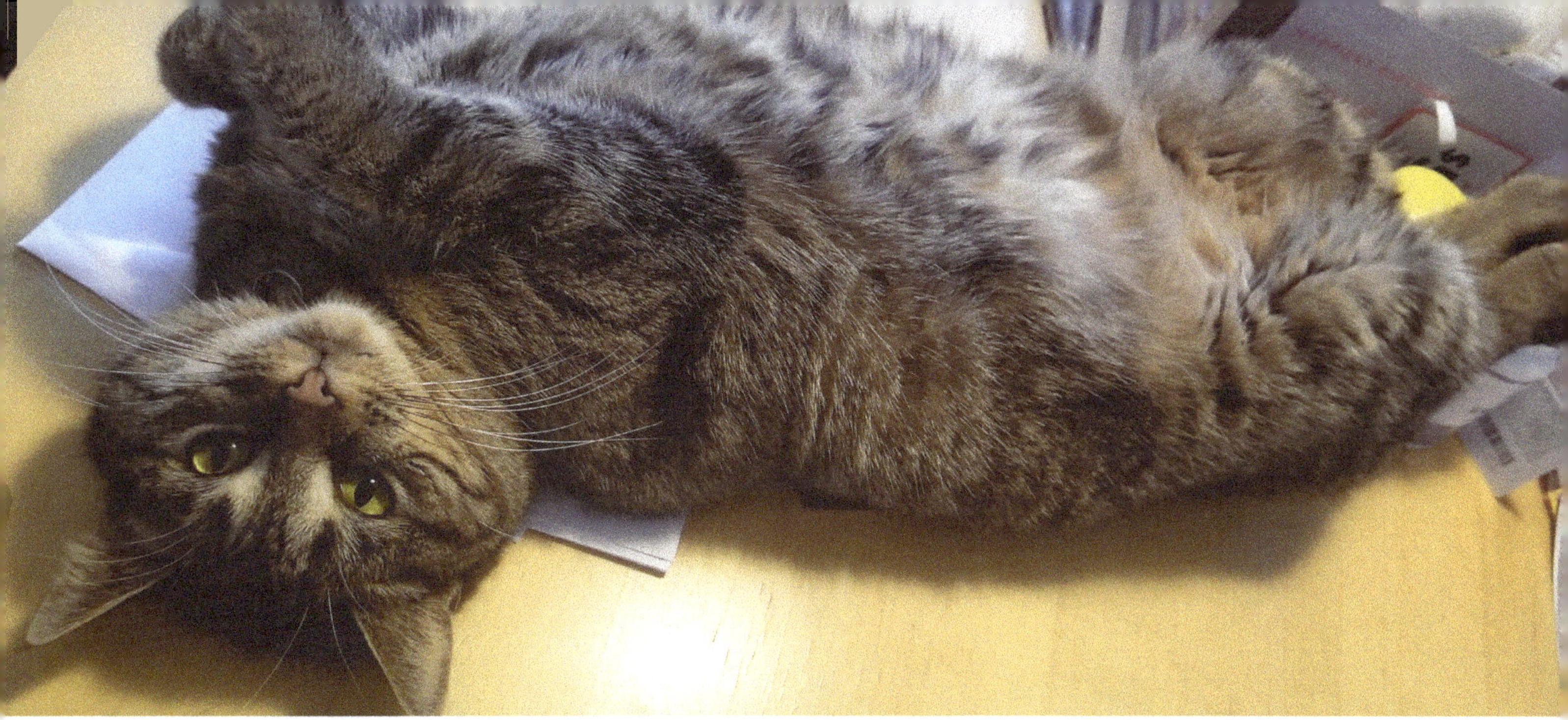

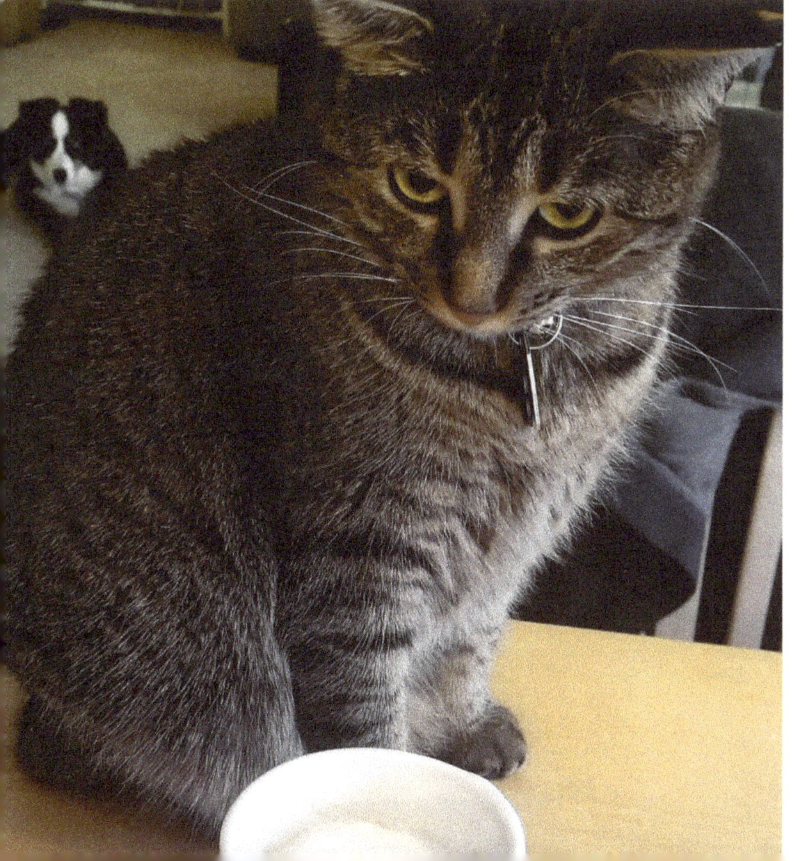

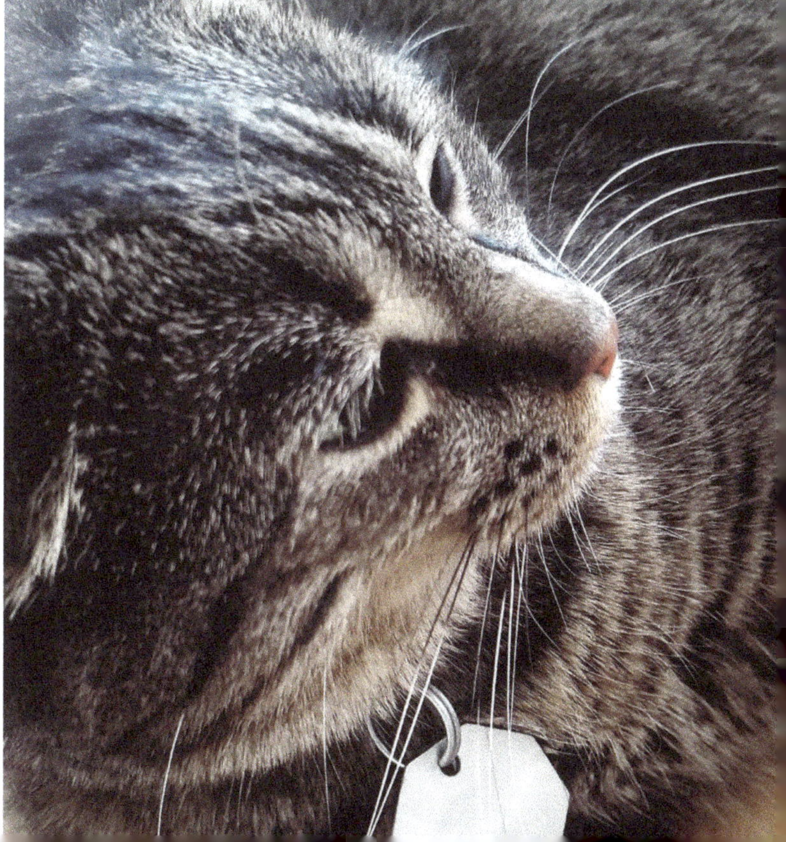

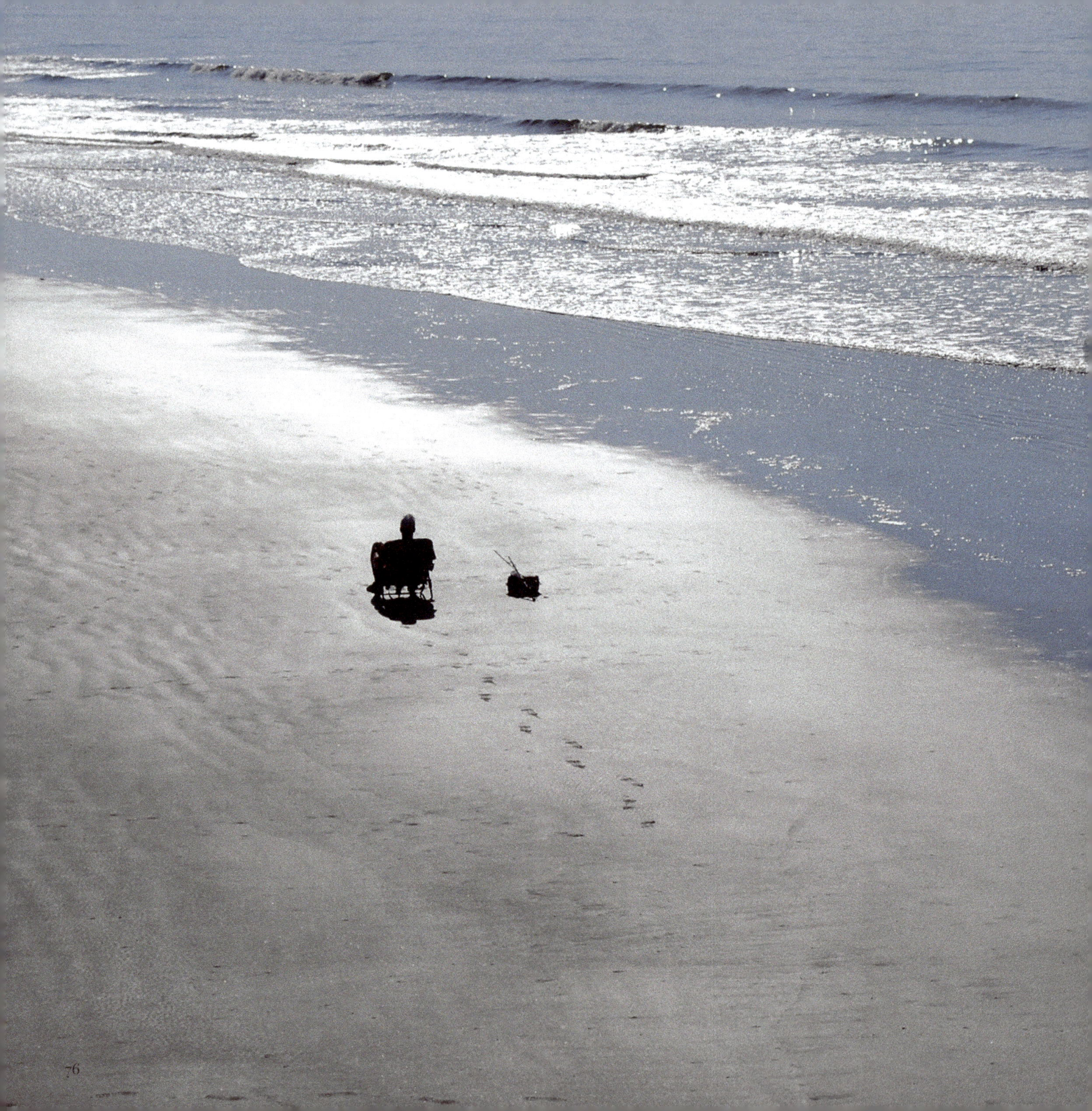

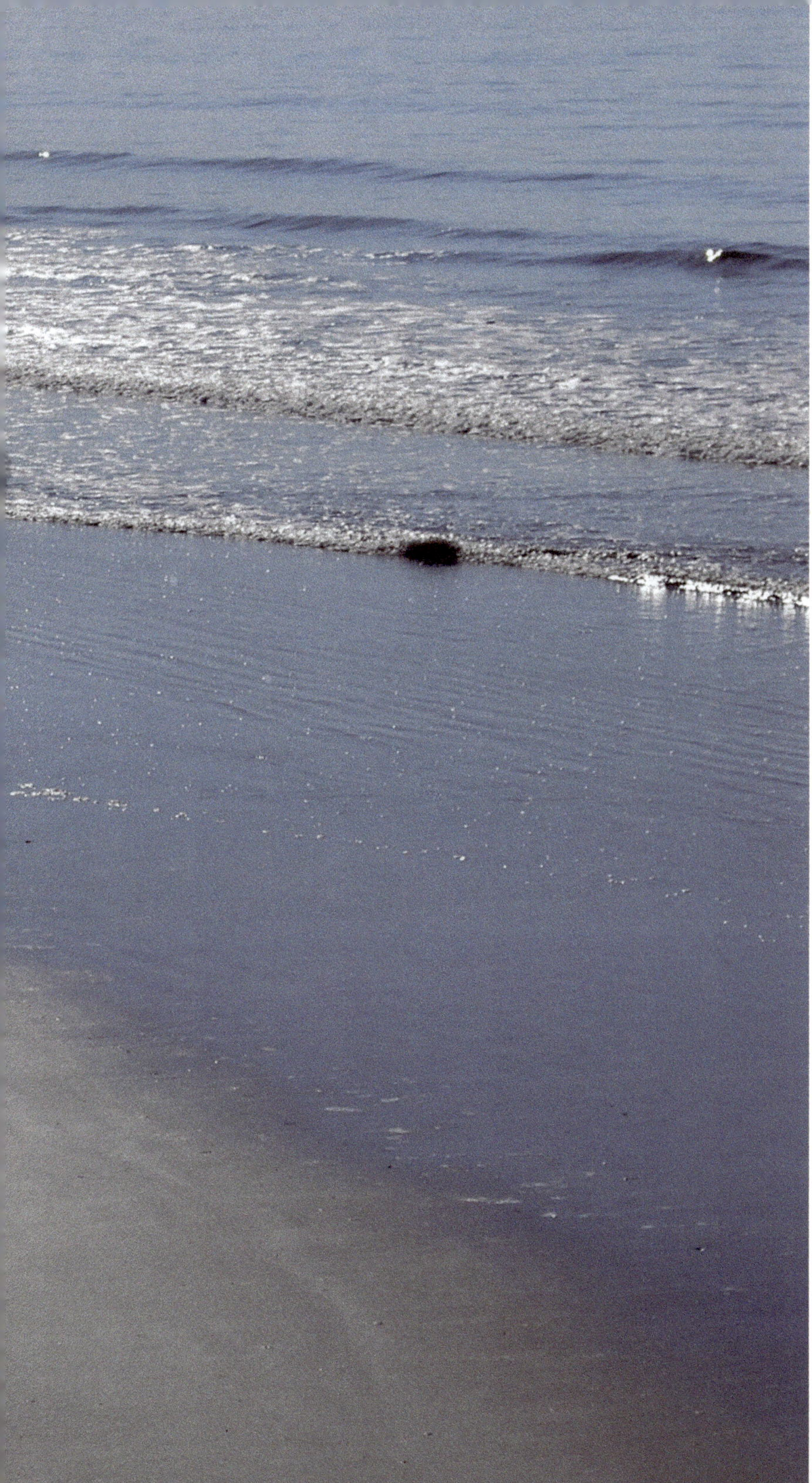

Morning Coffee

Sunshine at his back,
the angler reposes alongside
an opulent shoreline.
Waves imbricate,
murmuring secrets
of the deep.

Callused heels
permeate
the cool sand's
felicity.

With coffee in hand,
he's here to meditate.

Heron blue
and silver sea hues
provide a halcyon
retreat
replenishing
ineffable feelings of
well-being.

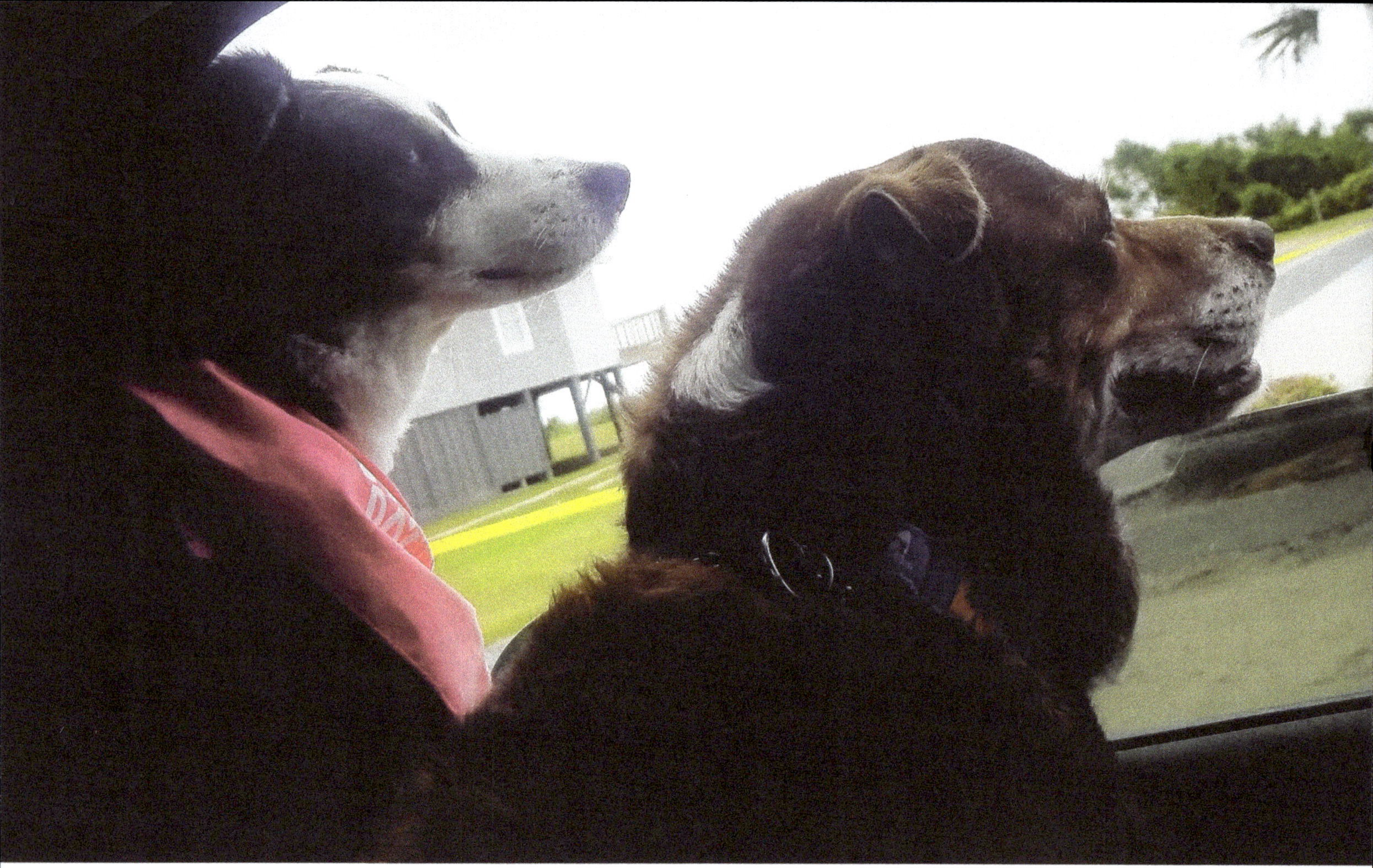

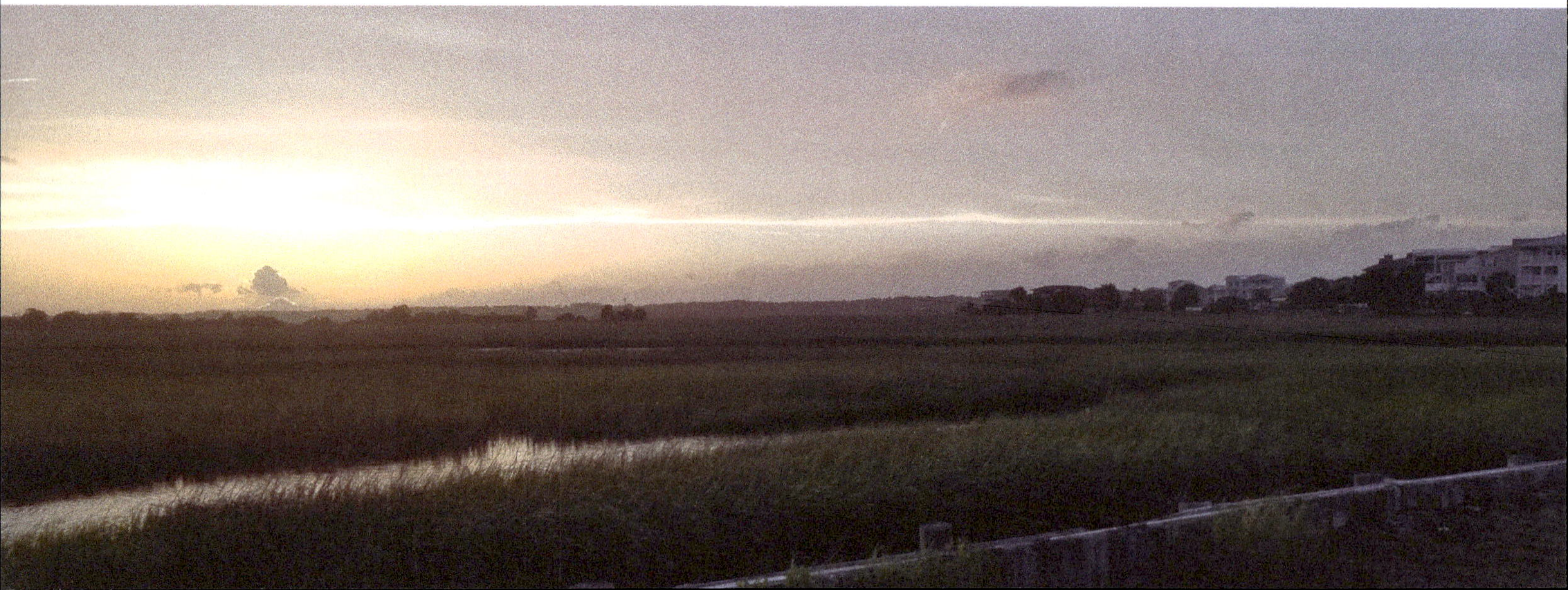

The Drift

Tails wag.
Furrows billow.
Red Dog and Pretty Dog
sniff narcissus,
pungent sea air,
and the scent of vacation
from the open window.

Crossing the connection
from mainland to island,
they eye
spindly-legged
white ibis,
peppery-headed wood storks
side-stepping in marsh shallows.

The aroma of caffeine concoctions
entices, like a genie in a bottle,
to climb a timbered stairway
and enter a surf-inspired café–
The Drift.

With soulful convincing eyes,
balancing on hind legs,
canine discerning palettes beg . . .
the last bits of a dulcet delight–
a cappuccino milkshake.

Tongues lap like ladles
calibrating trickles
of the creamy elixir
concealed in the
cup's crannies.

Coffee-flavored licks,
even sloppy kisses,
all free
for
the humans.

Coloring

Spilling over edges
of stark white pages
images of foxes and leaves
awaken
with waxy
sepia, mahogany, tumbleweed
hues.

The warmth of a lapis lazuli mug fits
perfectly
inside my palms, hiding lines . . .
evidence of
adventure and wisdom.

Peaks of fluffy whip cream . . .
evocative
of the Sangre De Cristo
Mountains after a
snowfall.

I gently
scribble my morning
away.

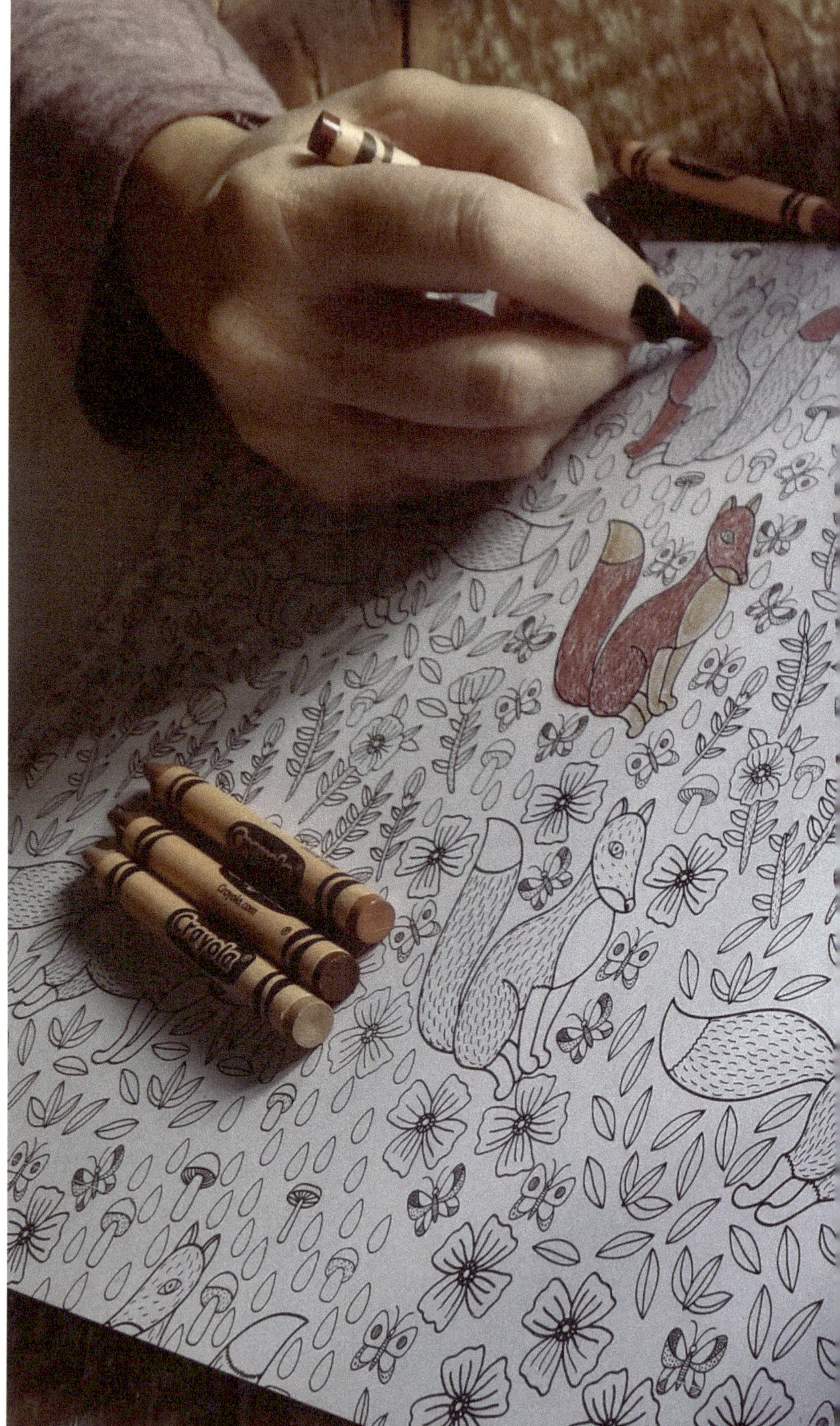

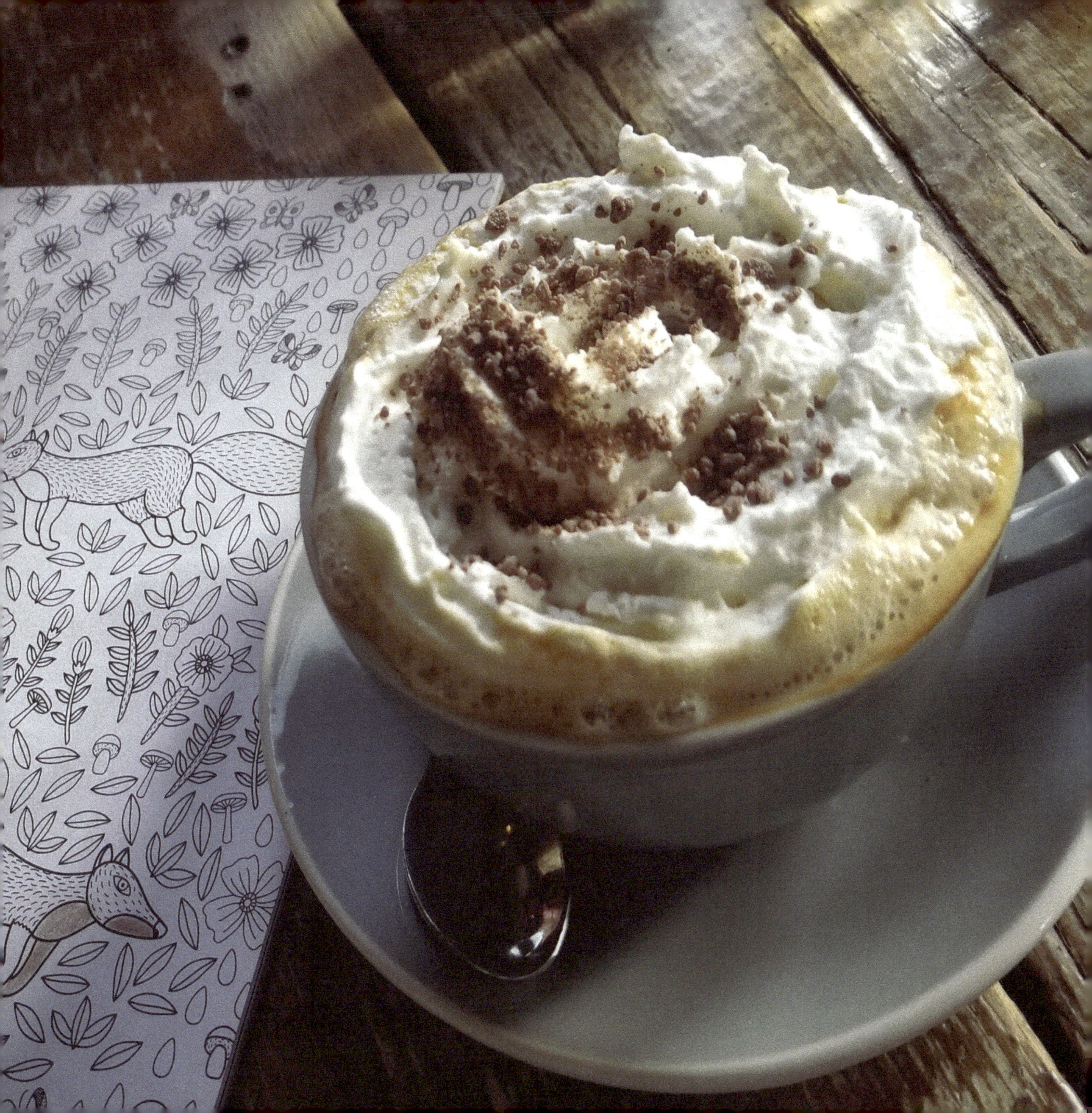

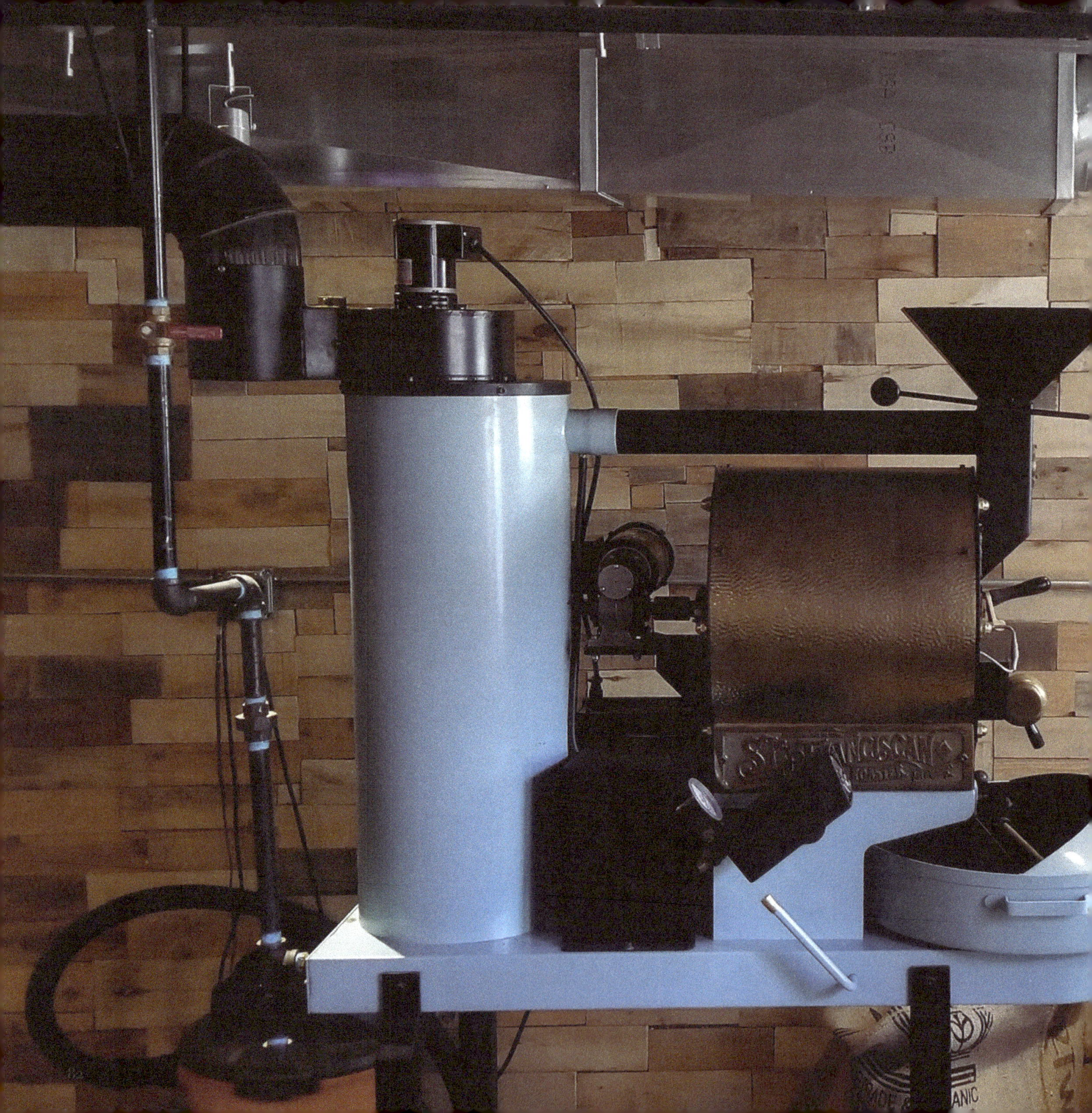

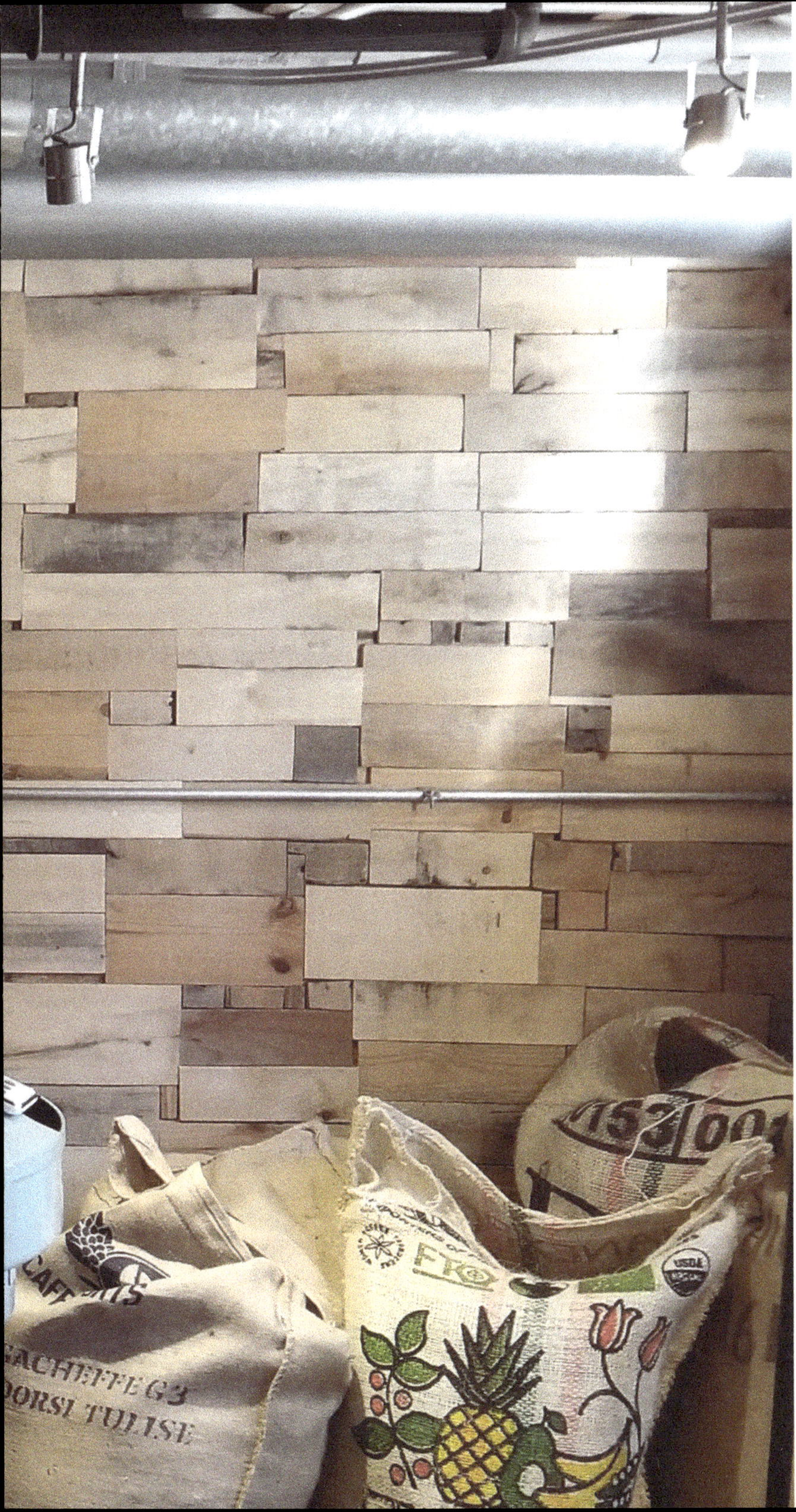

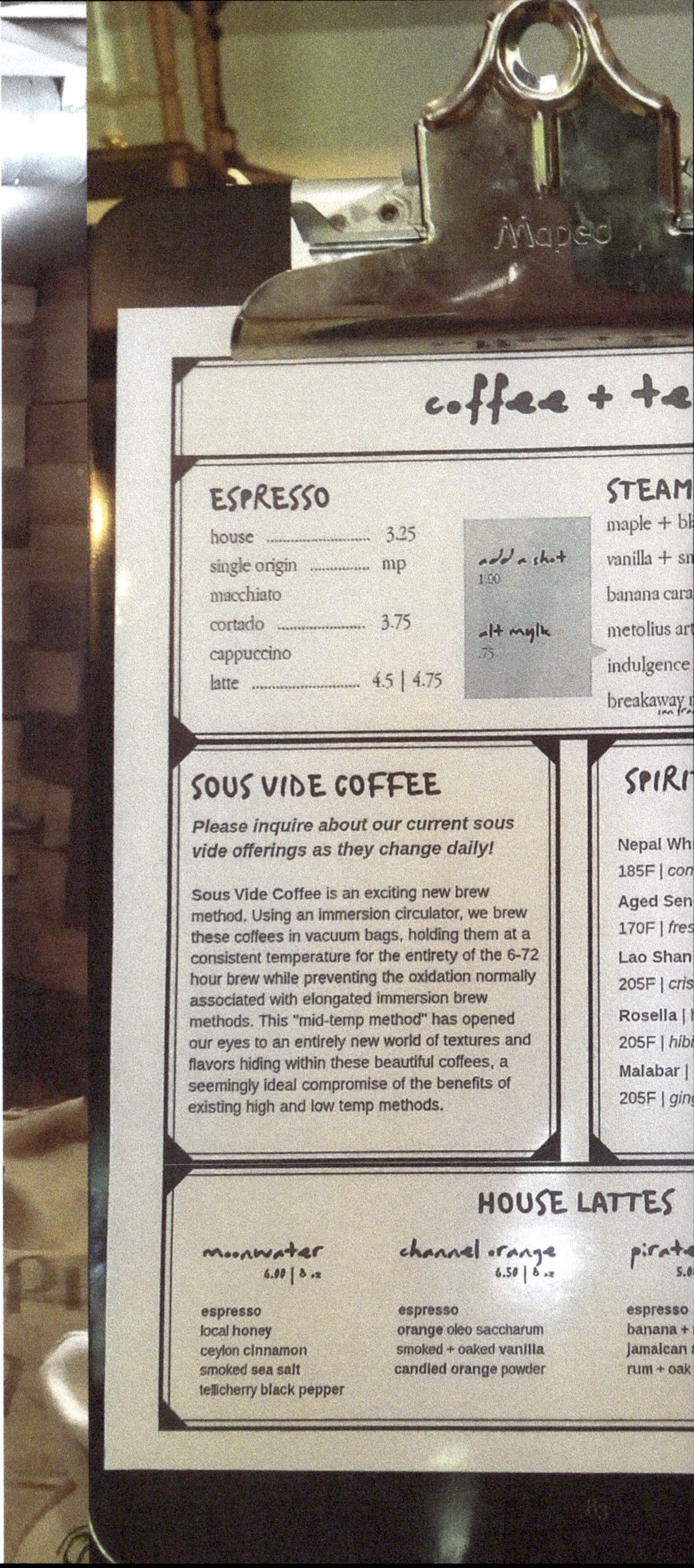

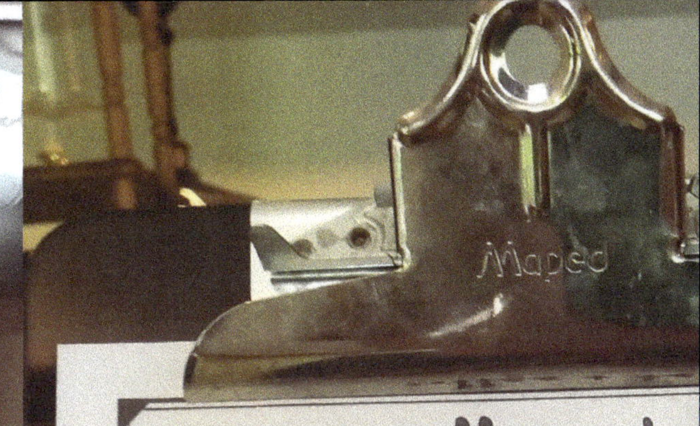
Maped
coffee +
ESPRESSO
house 3.25
single origin mp
macchiato
cortado 3.75
cappuccino
latte 4.5 | 4.75
add a shot 1.00
alt mylk .75
indulgence
SOUS VIDE COFFEE
Please inquire about our current sous vide offerings as they change daily!
Sous Vide Coffee is an exciting new brew method. Using an immersion circulator, we brew these coffees in vacuum bags, holding them at a consistent temperature for the entirety of the 6-72 hour brew while preventing the oxidation normally associated with elongated immersion brew methods. This "mid-temp method" has opened our eyes to an entirely new world of textures and flavors hiding within these beautiful coffees, a seemingly ideal compromise of the benefits of existing high and low temp methods.
185F
170F
Lao Shan
205F
Rosella
205F
Malabar
205F
HOUSE LATTES
moonwater
6.00 | 8 oz
espresso
local honey
ceylon cinnamon
smoked sea salt
tellicherry black pepper
channel orange
6.50 | 8 oz
espresso
orange oleo saccharum
smoked + oaked vanilla
candied orange powder
espresso

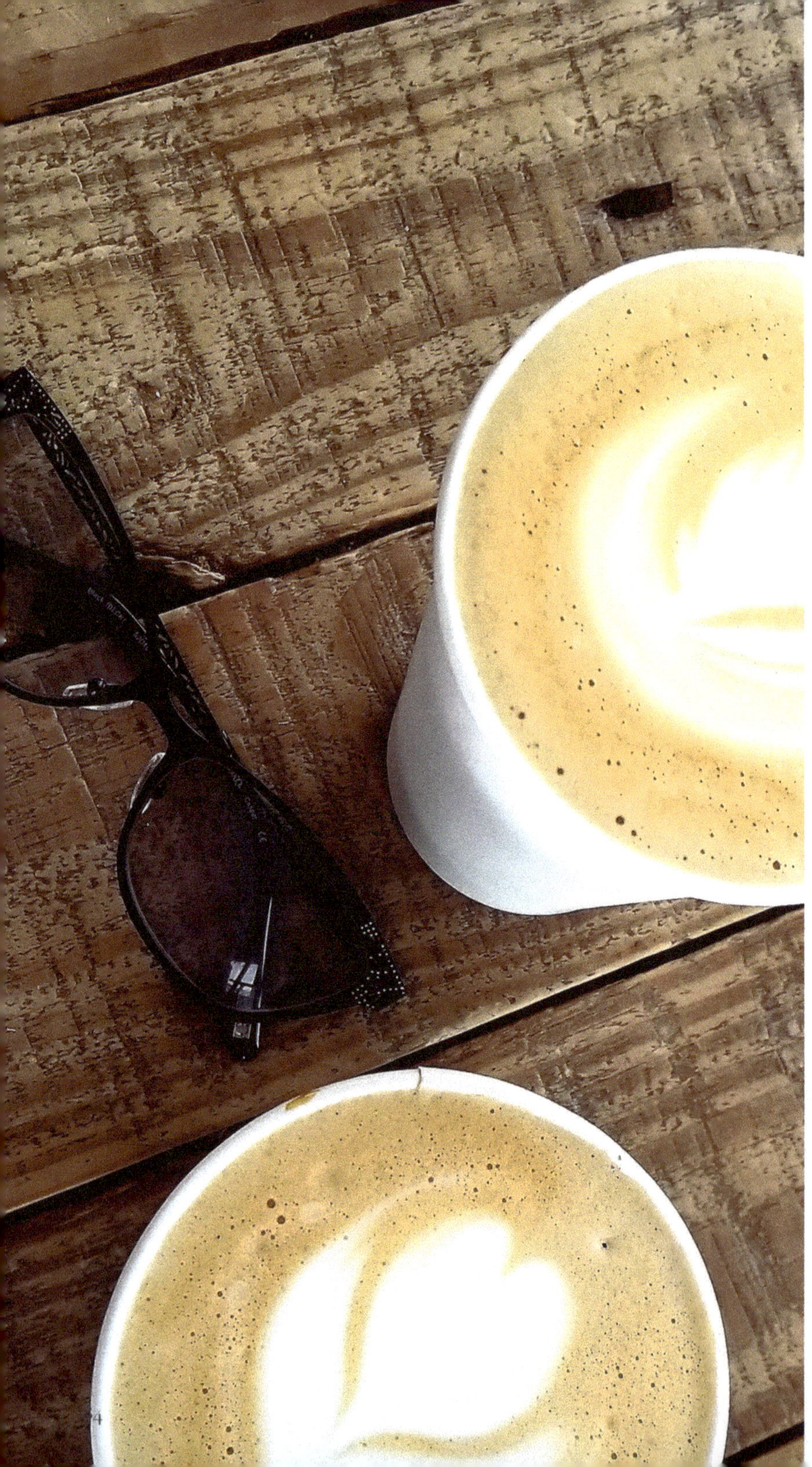

The Meeting

A fifty-something
silver fox
with olive green eyes
rests adjacent
to a Jenna Elfman look-alike.

In the midst of
documents
strewn about the table,
two to-go cups
anchor the encounter.

Distraught,
the well-manicured
woman,
in tan form-fitting top,
designer jeans,
and beige stilettos,
squawks, scribbles, motions,
frantically
rustling papers.

He listens.
Still.
Cool.
Stoic.

Pausing
frequently,
she sips liquid
energy from
the paper cup.

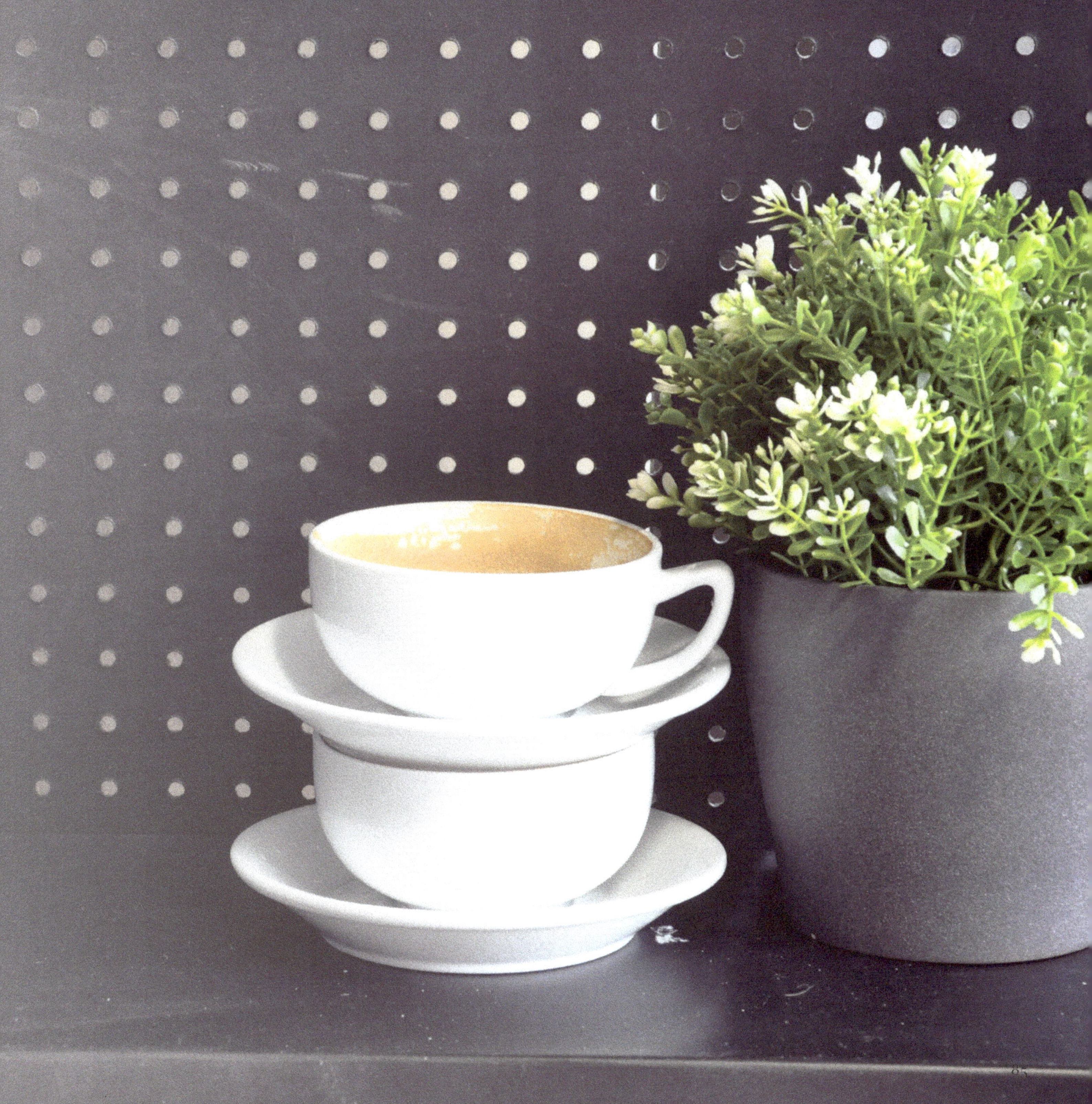

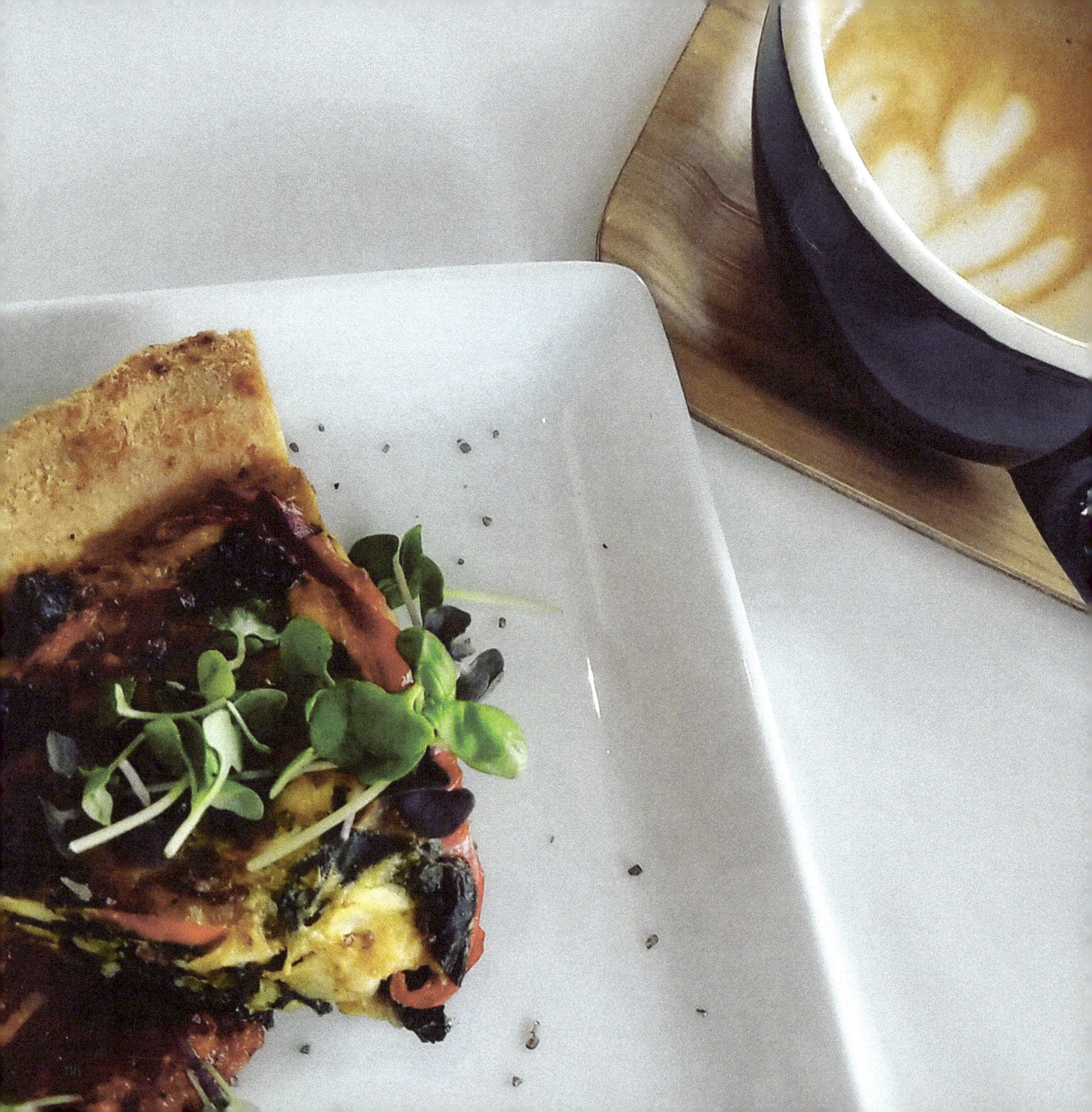

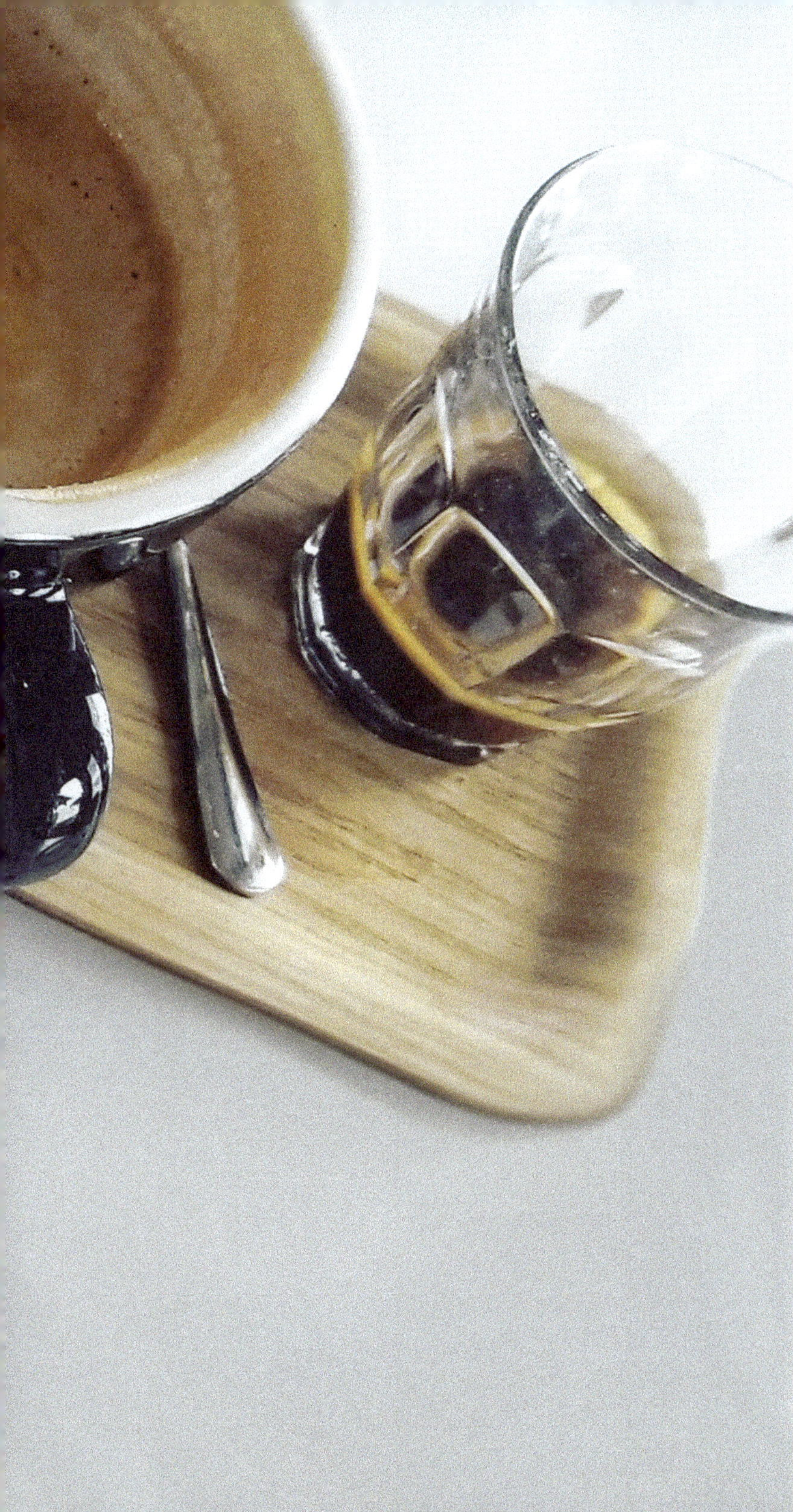

Going Separate Ways

You step lightly
as you saunter through the doorway
of our favorite café...

Upon your approach, you grin and ask,
"How are you?"
You take a seat
at the counter.
We reminisce
over coffee.

The aroma
of crispy hash browns, maple sausage,
and Vidalia onions emanate from the grill,
and soft sounds of smooth jazz
make our conversation
a little easier.

You ask about my plans,
as if you really care.

We sip another coffee,
laughing about that time in St. Croix
we fed the pigs beer.

"It was a special time,"
as I gently ease the manila envelope
across the metal counter.

Always, with infectious dimples you chuckle,
"At least we'll have breakfast at Tiffany's."

But I couldn't tell if you were being sincere,
because you never were . . .

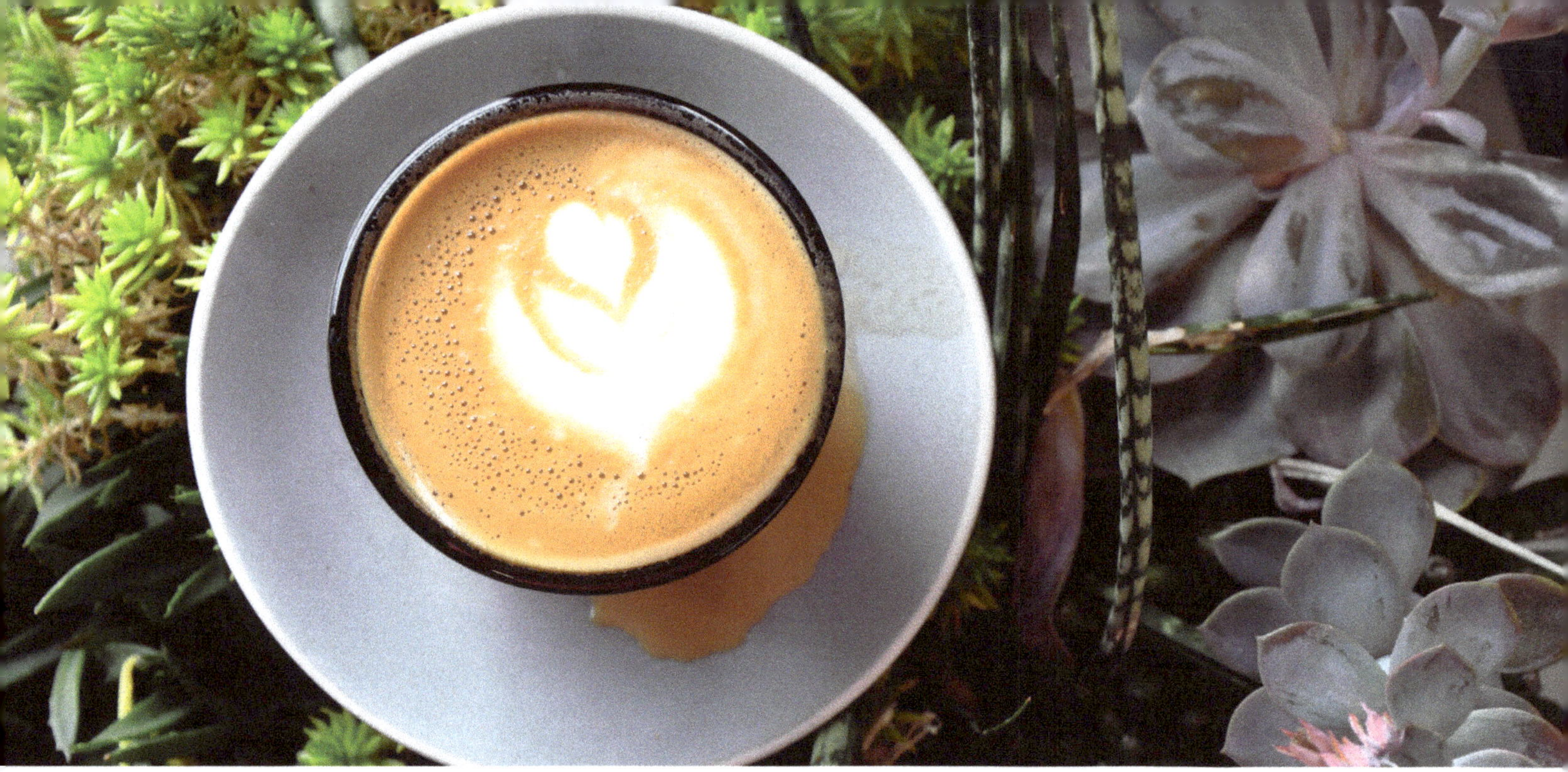

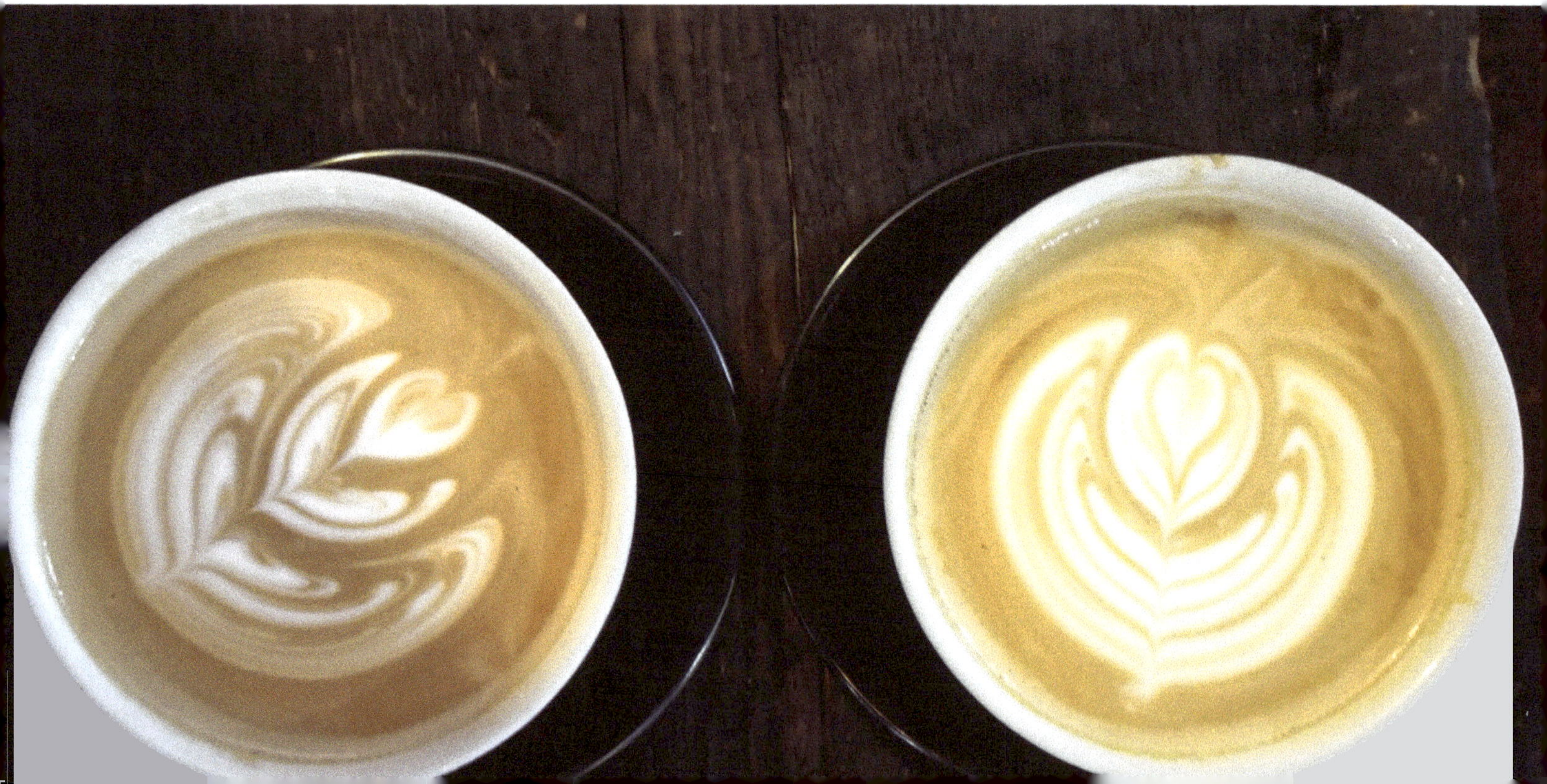

Coffee Coma

(life after coronavirus)

After this social distancing
'thing'
is over –
an unavoidable journey
of wanderlust
to best-loved cafés,
with kindred spirits
and coffee aficionados.

Friend,
we'll sip
frothy lattes,
iced cappuccinos,
pretentious Americanos,
savor sumptuous espresso
martinis
and indulge in creamy
Affogatos,
until night falls
an autumnal cornucopia
of Mocha,
Café Au Lait,
and
Caramel Macchiatos.

We'll be as high
as a harvest moon
rising.

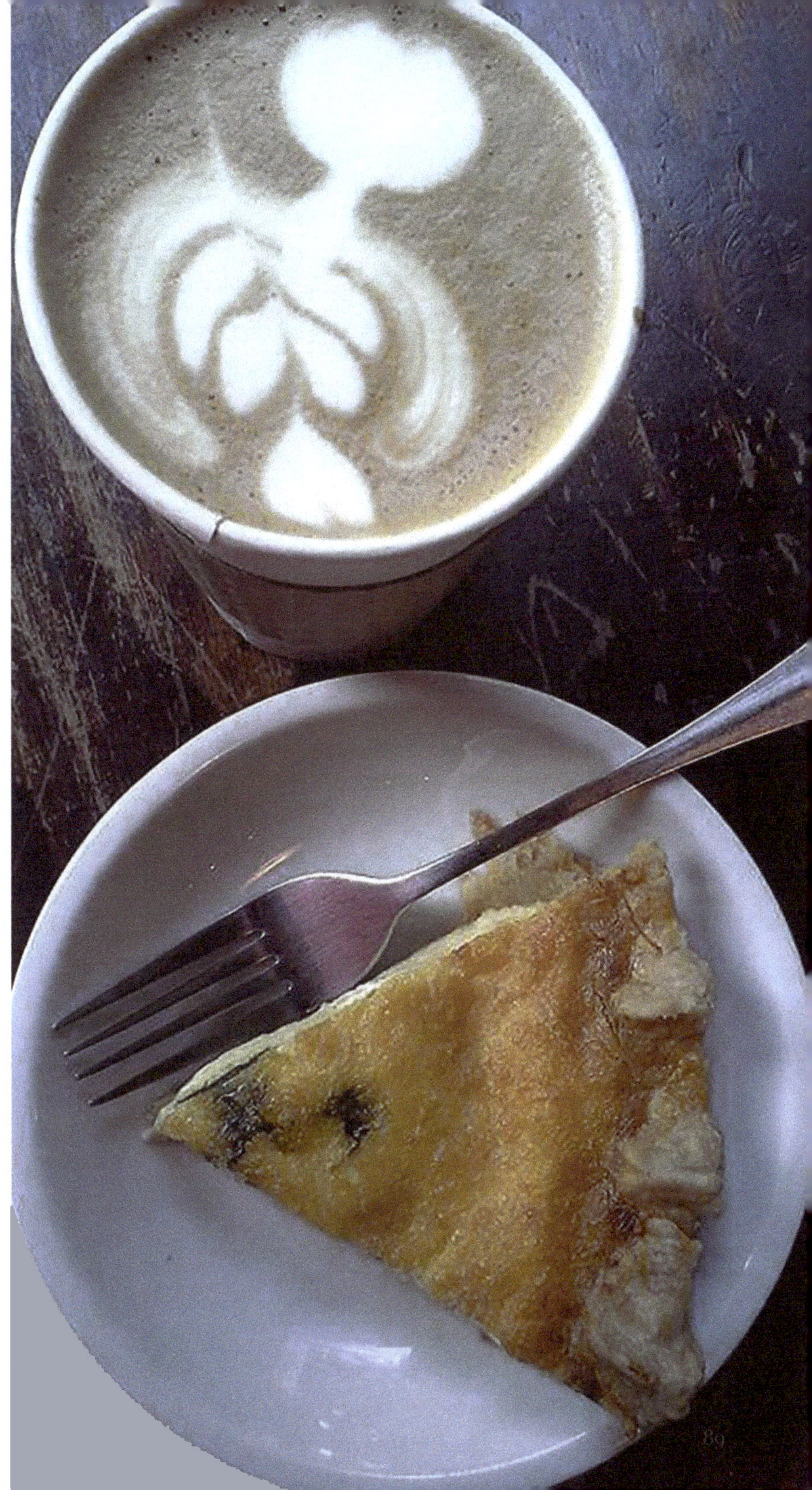

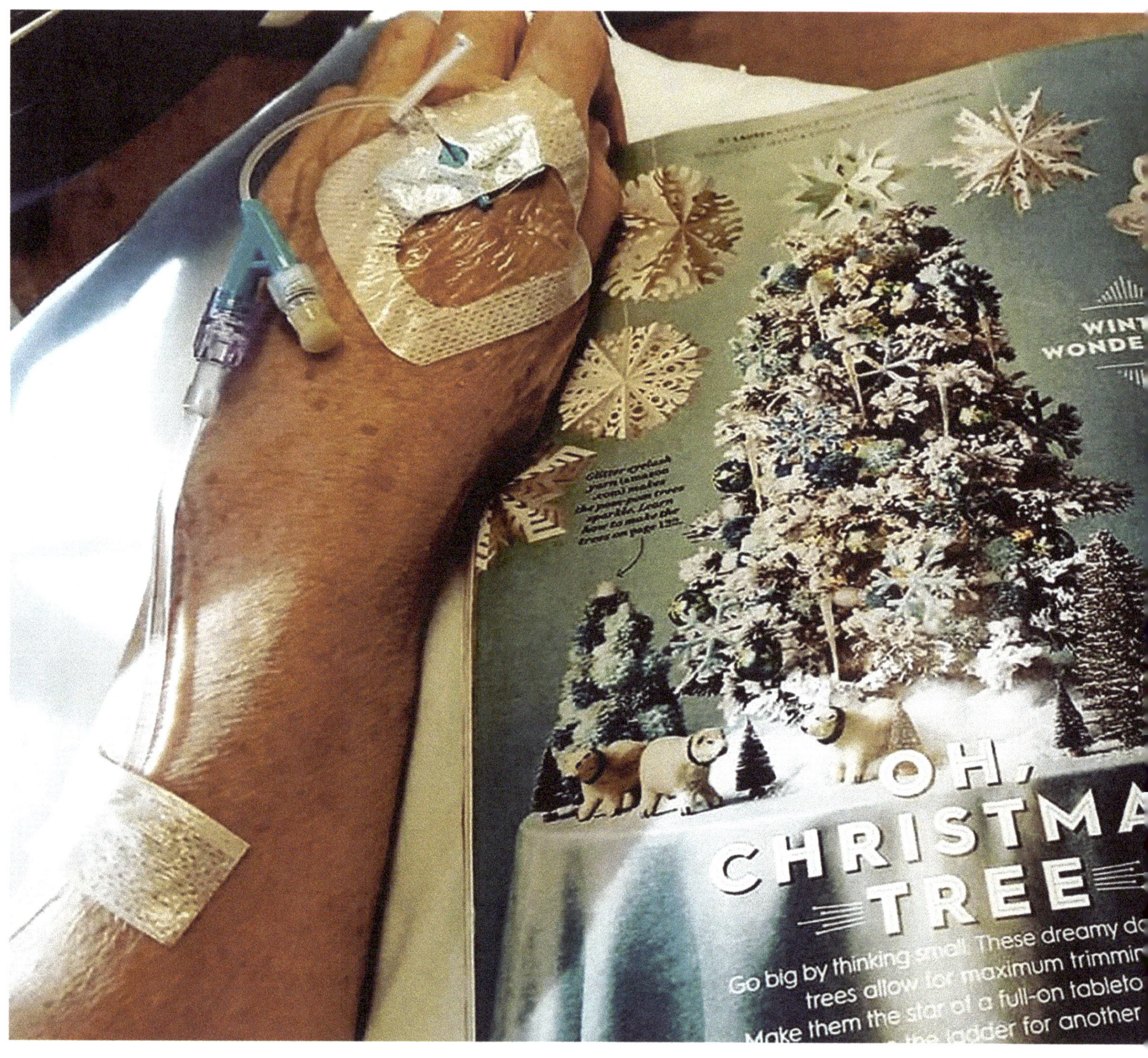

OH,
CHRISTMA
TREE
Go big by thinking small. These dreamy
trees allow for maximum
Make them the star of a full-on

No Caffeine Before Chemo

Resting weary bones
on the celadon leather chair
in the treatment room,
I casually sip a designer cappuccino
until
the charge nurse threads
the cannula into
my forearm.

Flushed and anxious,
I look away.

On her third attempt
she emphasizes,
"No caffeine before chemo–
it constricts
the veins."

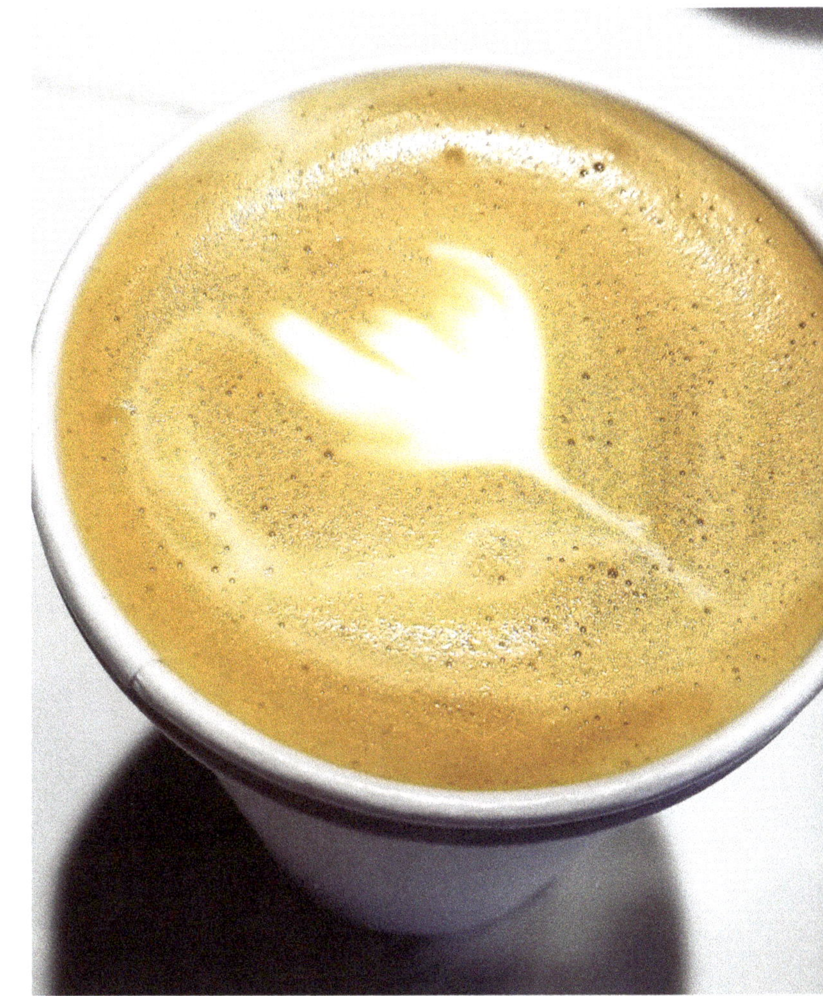

When I Was Seventeen

In a forest of pine
and oak,
flames crackle and embers glow.
The scent of coffee mingles with smoke.

A speckled
blue enamel coffee pot
mimics hues of stars and sky,
bubbles and boils like a volcano,
roasting over the heart of the fire.

Conversations we held
when I was
seventeen.

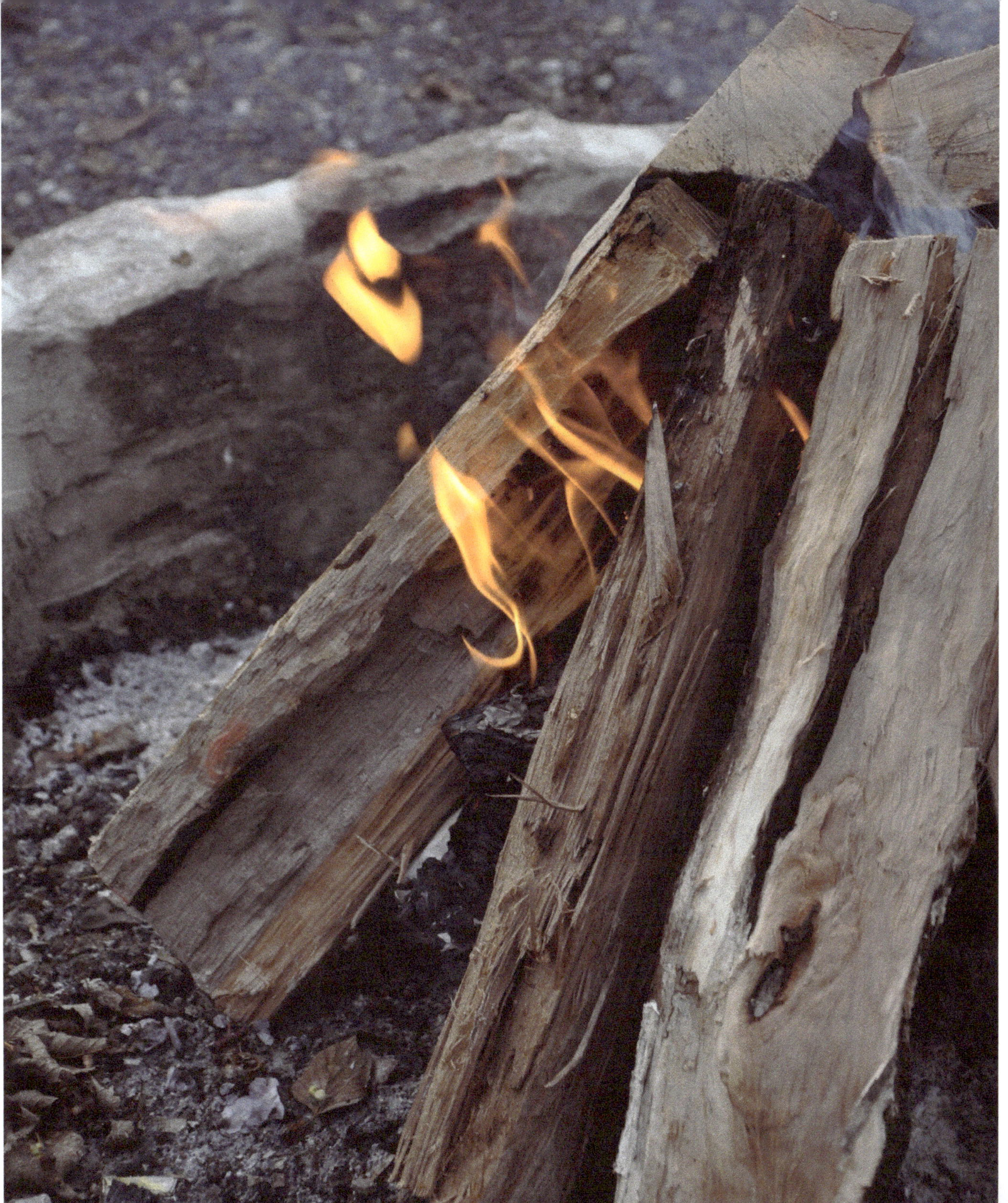

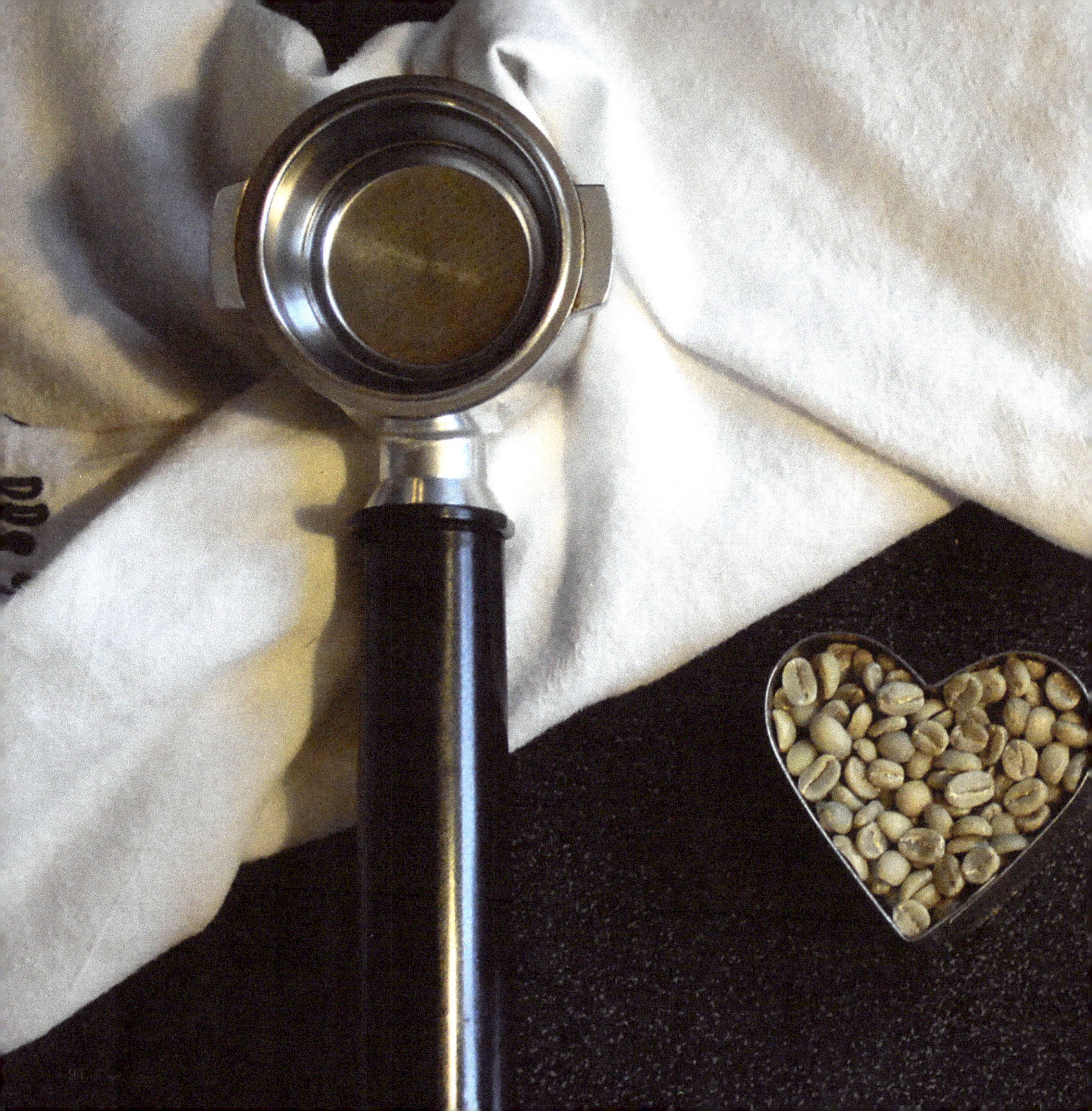

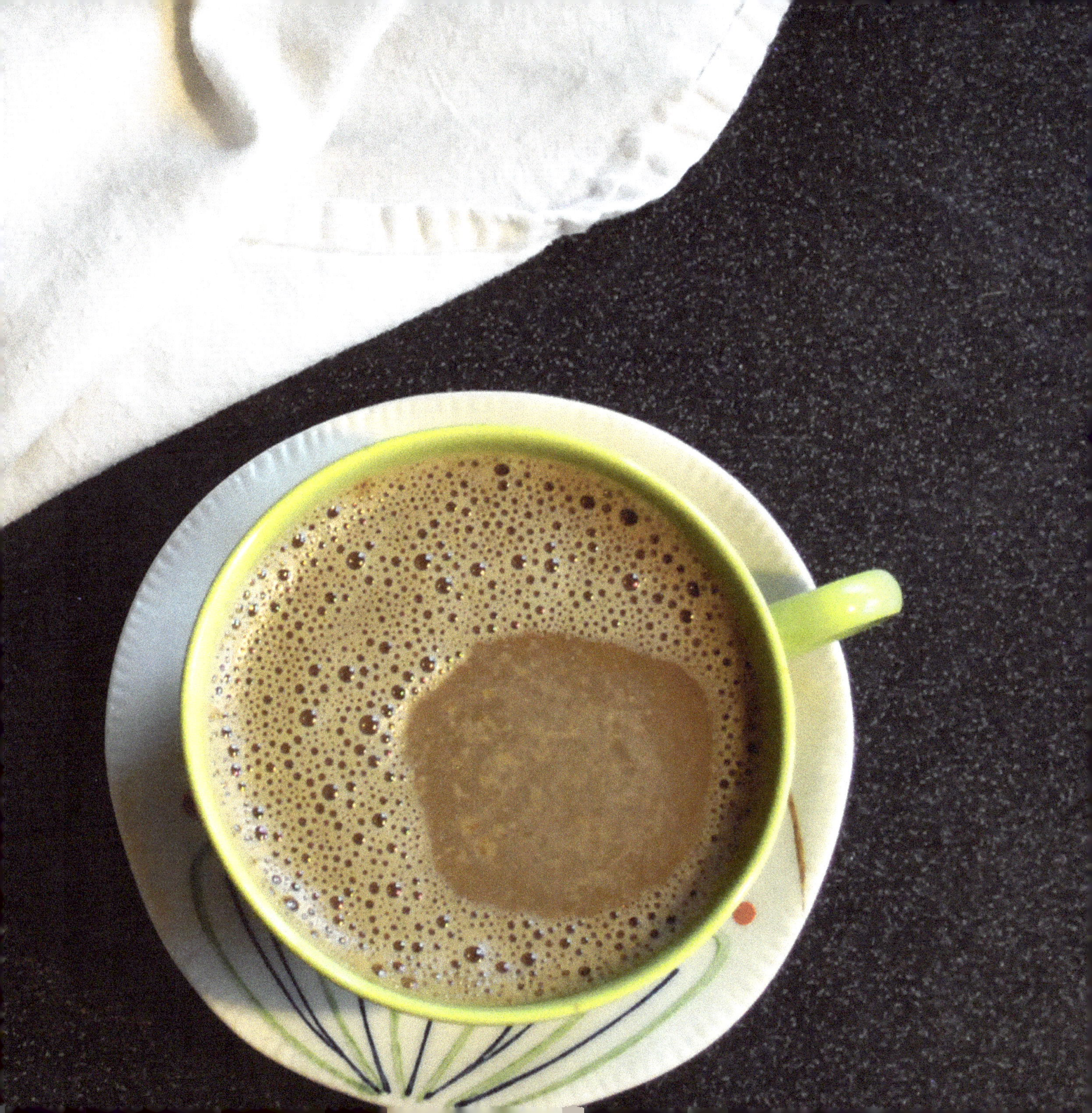

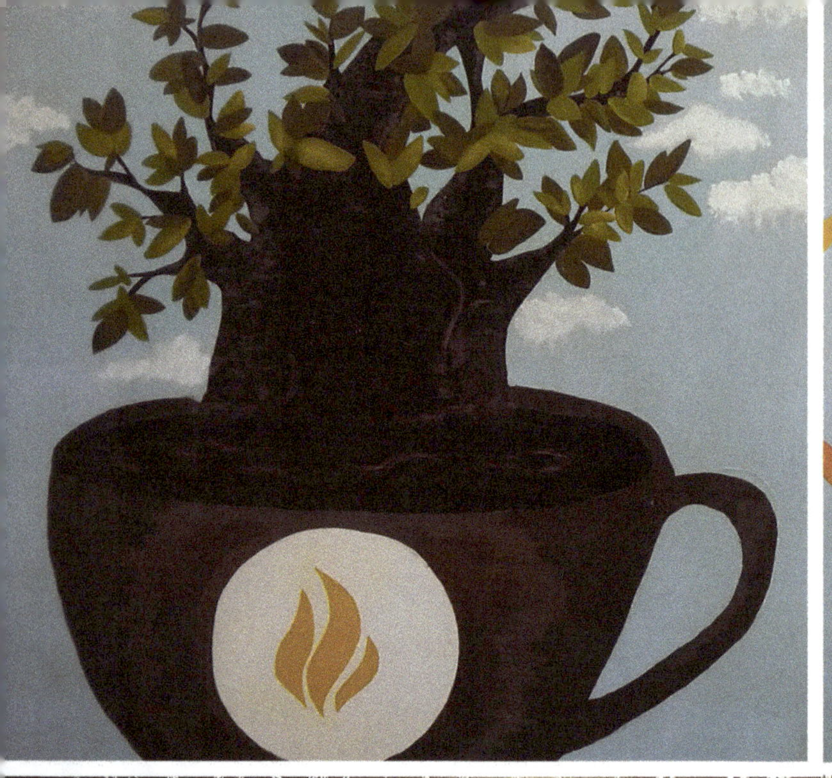

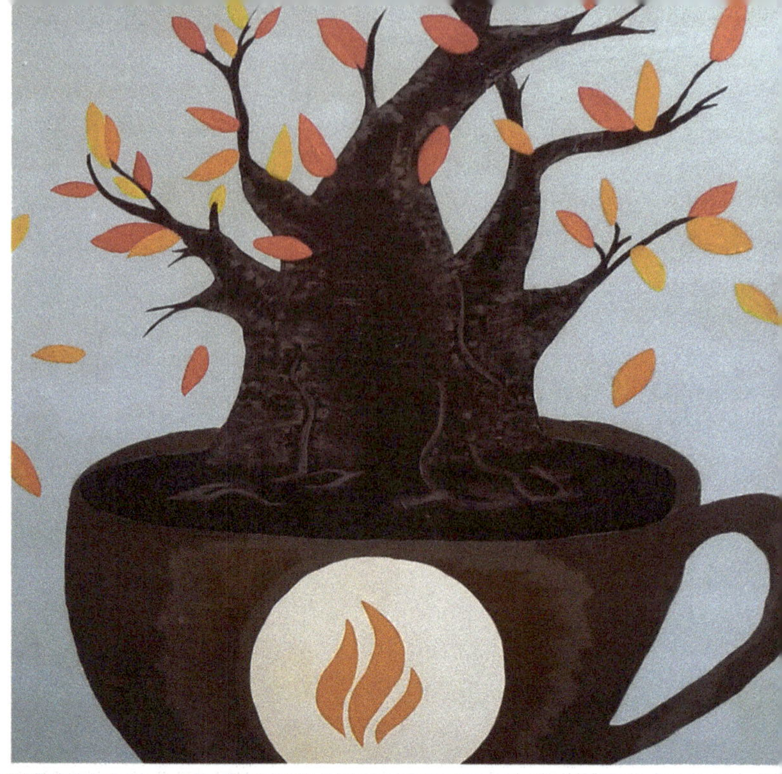

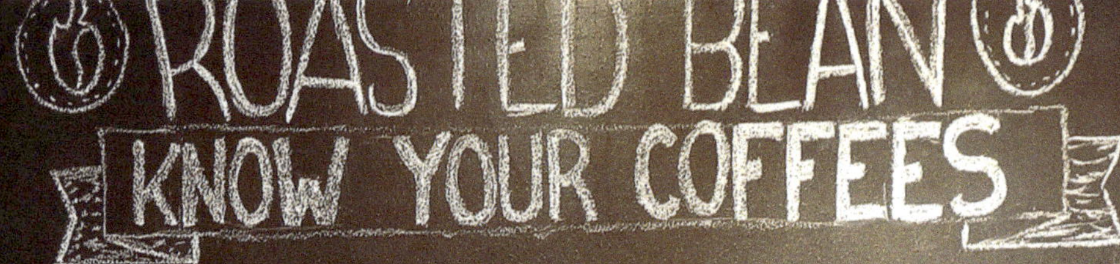
ROASTED BEAN
KNOW YOUR COFFEES

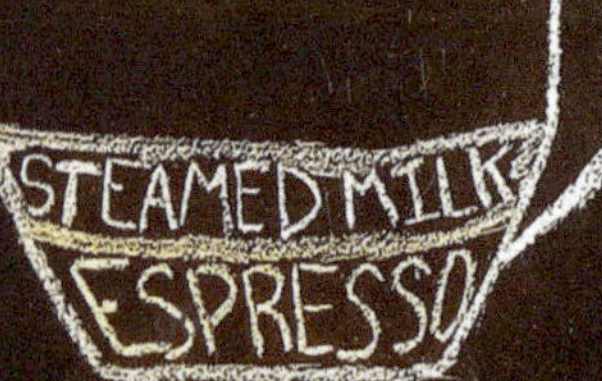
ESPRESSO
Espresso
BREWED COFFEE
Drip Coffee
HOT WATER
ESPRESSO
Americano
STEAMED MILK
ESPRESSO
MILK FOAM
STEAMED MILK
ESPRESSO
STEAMED MILK
ESPRESSO

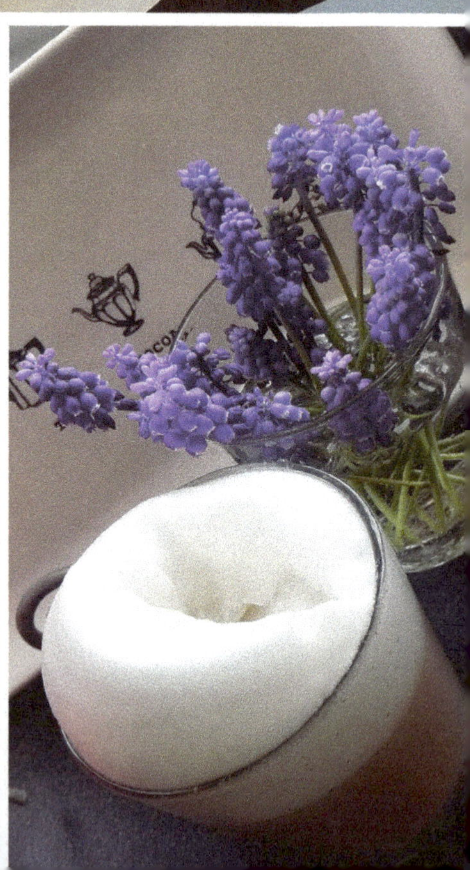

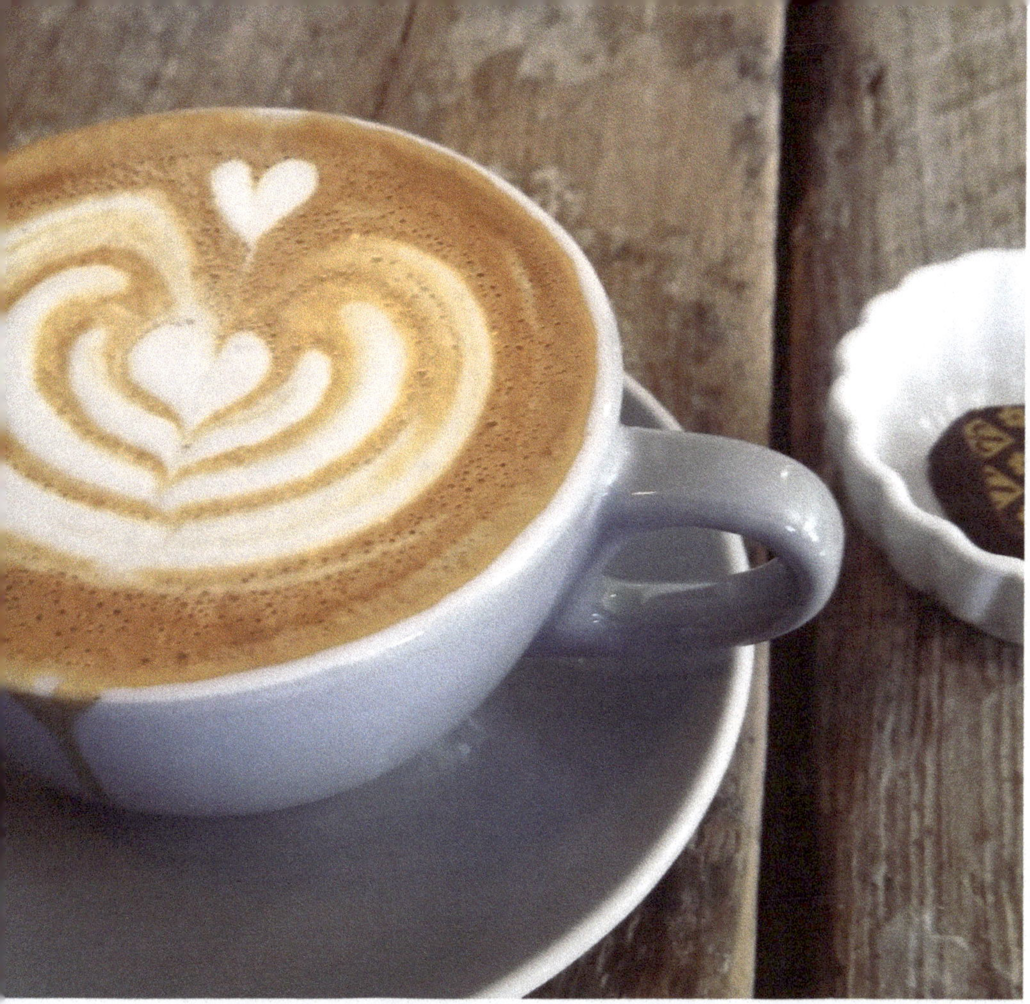

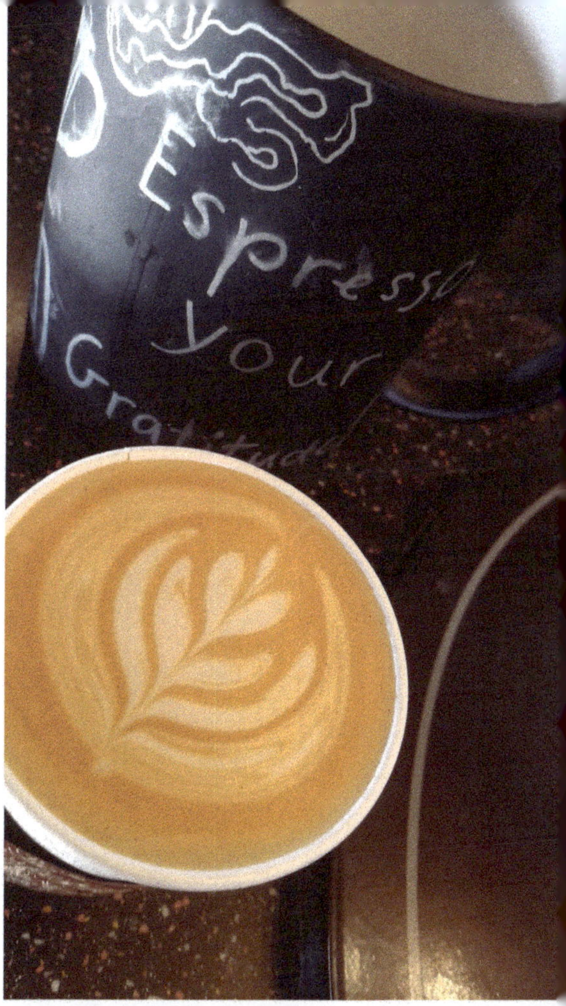

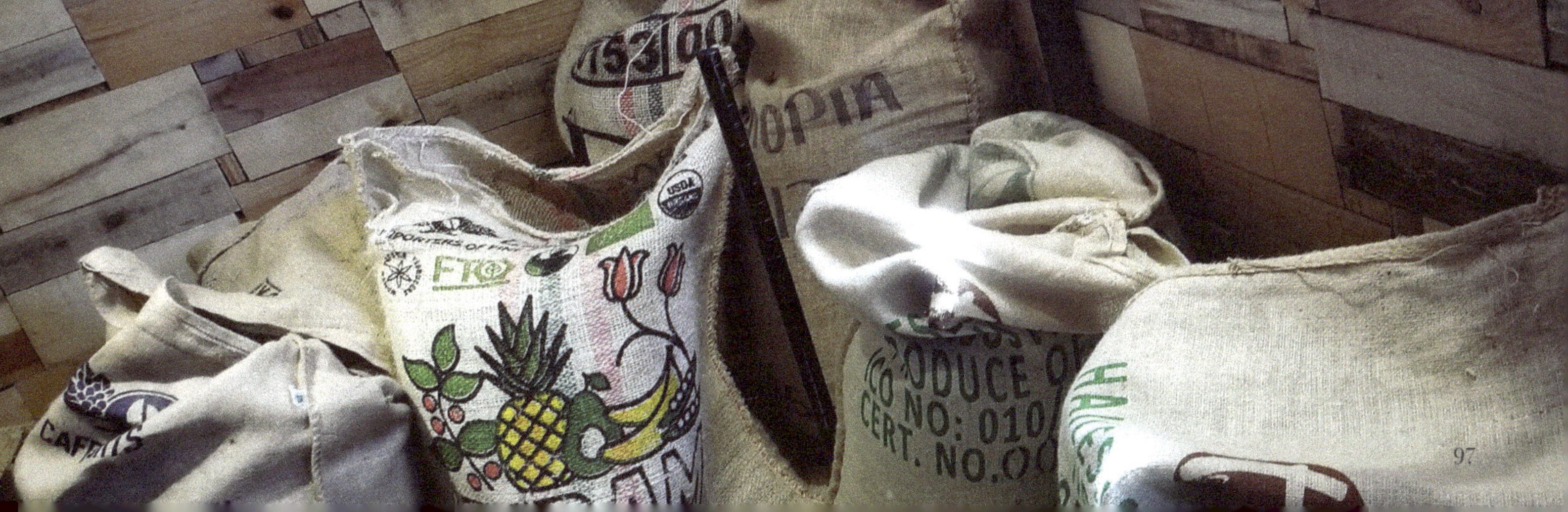

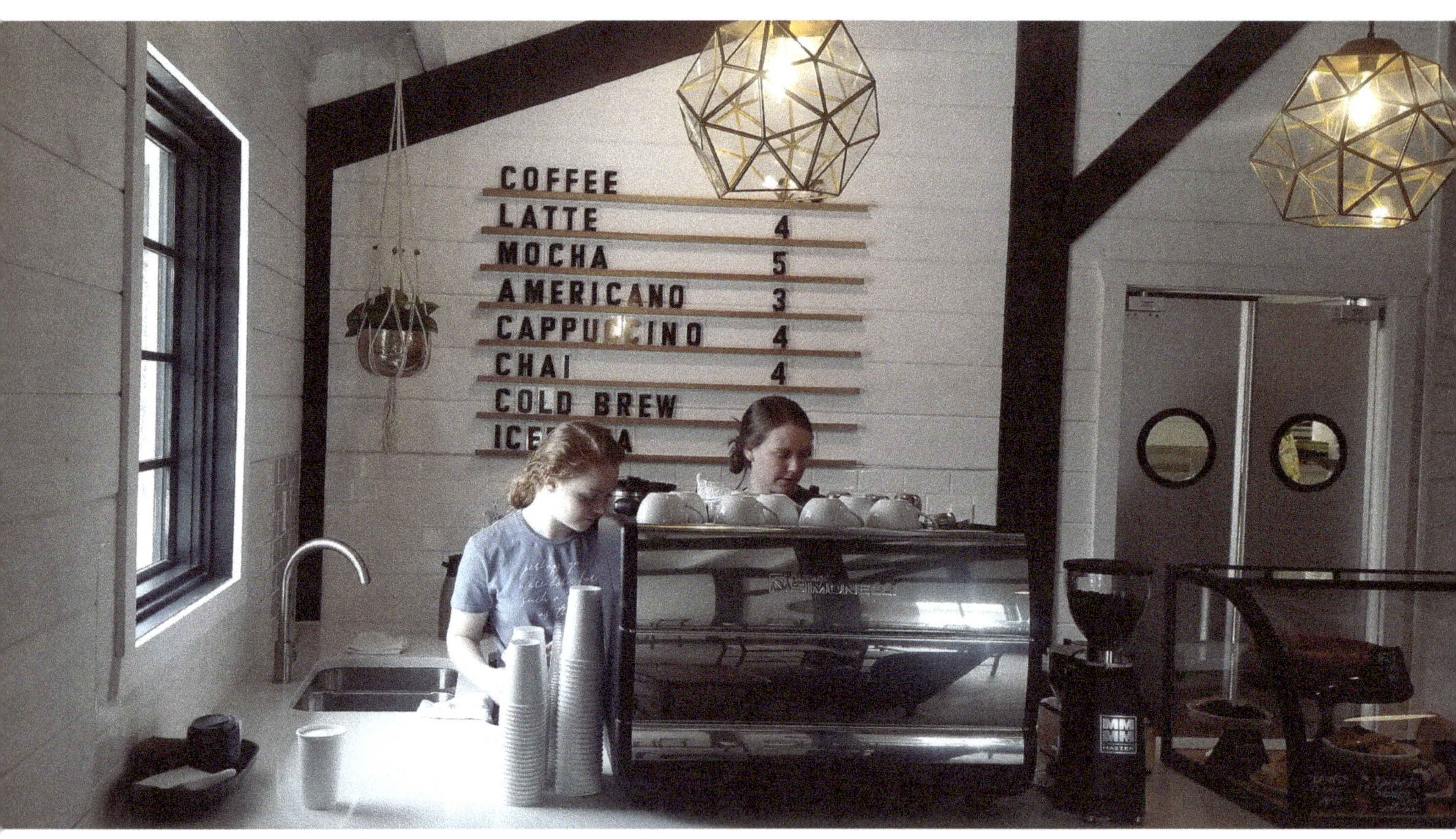
COFFEE
LATTE 4
MOCHA 5
AMERICANO 3
CAPPUCCINO 4
CHAI 4
COLD BREW

Sheree's Favorite Coffeehouses

representing thirteen states and two locations in the Caribbean

If you have a favorite coffeehouse you think Sheree should visit, drop her an email at shereenielsen@gmail.com.

ARKANSAS

Nexus Coffee Creative
301B President Clinton Ave
Little Rock AR 72201
(501) 295-7515

CALIFORNIA

Caffe Luxxe
22333 CA-1
Suite 160
Malibu CA 90265
(310) 394-2222

Grill at Point Pinos
(formerly Crema PG)
77 Asilomar
Pacific Grove CA 93950
(831) 375-1313

Malibu Farm Pier Café
23000 Pacific Coast Hwy
Malibu CA 90265
(310) 456-1112

Simply Coffee
940 N Lima St
Burbank CA 91505
(818) 394-6831

Tidal Coffee
400 Cannery Row
Monterey CA 93940
(831) 645-4030

FLORIDA

Amavida Coffee and Tea
104 N Barrett Square #1A
Rosemary Beach FL 32461
(850) 213-1965

Capriccio Café
810 Hwy 98 East
Destin FL 32541
(850) 460-7050

GEORGIA

Tybee Art and Coffee Bar
1213 Old US Hwy 80
Tybee Island GA 31328
(912) 224-5227

HAWAII

Bella Surf
640 Front St
Lahaina HI 96761
(808) 446-3709

Kai Coffee Hawaii at Alohilani Resort
2490 Kalakaua Ave
Suite #131
Honolulu HI 96815
(808) 926-1131

Kai Coffee Hawaii at Hyatt Regency
2424 Kalakaua Ave
Honolulu HI 96815
(808) 923-1700

ILLINOIS

Coffee Hound
407 North Main
Bloomington IL 61701
(309) 827-7575

River Coffee Company
101 N Main St
Decatur IL 62523
(217) 454-2905

KENTUCKY

Sunergos (p. 14, bottom left)
306 West Woodlawn
Louisville KY 40214
(502) 368-2820

MISSISSIPPI

Bright-Eyed Brew Co (p. 43)
623 Washington Ave
Ocean Springs MS 39564
(228) 297-2268

MISSOURI

Course Coffee Roasters (p. 103)
1218 N 2nd St
St Charles MO 63301
(217) 481-6244

Foundation Grounds
7298 Manchester Rd
Maplewood MO 63143
(314) 833-6460

Kaldis Coffee
17211 Chesterfield Airport Rd
Chesterfield MO 63005
(636) 536-6624

Lakota Coffee
24 S 9th St
Columbia MO 65201
(573) 874-2852

Long Row Lavender (p. 98)
26549 S Stracks Church Rd
Wright City MO 63390
(636) 699-0690

Maypop Coffee and Garden Shop
803 Marshall Ave
Webster Groves MO 63119
(314) 764-2140

Picasso's
101 N Main St
St Charles MO 63301
(636) 925-2911

Roasted Bean (p. 98)
441 Main St.
Troy MO 63379
(636) 775-2566

Shortwave Coffee (pp. 2, 42, & 82)
915 Alley A
Columbia MO 65201
(573) 214-0880

Sump Coffee (p. 14, center left)
3700 S Jefferson Ave
St. Louis MO 63118
(917) 412-5670

The Living Room (p. 44)
2808 Sutton Blvd
Maplewood MO 63143
(314) 899-0173

Upshot Coffee (p. 14, top right)
5326 Highway N
St Charles MO 63304
(636) 352-1139

Upshot Brake Shop (p. 26)
816 N Kingshighway St
St Charles MO 63301
(636) 209-4331

Yanis Coffee Zone
130 E High St
Jefferson City MO 65101
(573) 761-4277

NORTH CAROLINA

Drift
20 E Second St
Ocean Isle Beach NC 28469
(910) 579-3664

Liberty House Coffee & Café
221 South Liberty St
Asheville NC 28801
(828) 505 2236

Magic Bean Coffee Bazaar
35 School Rd
Ocracoke NC 27960
(252) 588-2440

Morning Times
10 E Hargett St
Raleigh NC 27601
(919) 836-1204

Panacea Coffee Company
66 Commerce St
Waynesville NC 28756-5738
(828) 452-6200

SOUTH CAROLINA

Kudu Coffee and Beer
4 Vanderhorst St
Charleston SC 29403
(843) 853-7186

Lost Dog Café
106 W Huron Ave
Folly Beach SC 29439
(843) 588-9669

TENNESSEE

8th and Roast
2108 8th Ave S
Nashville TN 37204
(615) 730-8074

Black Press Coffee
115 Walton Ferry Rd #20
Hendersonville TN 37075
(615) 604-0021

Frothy Monkey
2509 12th Ave S
Nashville TN 37204
(615) 600-4756

Frothy Monkey
125 5th Ave S
Franklin TN 37064
(615) 600-4756

Honest Coffee Roasters
230 Franklin Rd
Suite 11A
Franklin TN 37064
(615) 807-1726

Plumb Line Coffee
124 University Ave
Clarksville TN 37040
(931) 896-2020

WISCONSIN

Bearded Heart
8093 WI-57
Baileys Harbor WI 54202
(920) 839-9111

Discourse Coffee:
A Liquid Workshop (p. 83)
5625 W. West Wells Street
Milwaukee WI 53213

Ephraim Coffee Lab
3055 Church St
Ephraim WI 54211

Java Dock
116 W Grand Ave
Suite 101
Port Washington WI 53074
(262) 284-1600

ST. JOHN, USVI

Papaya Café
The Marketplace
Saint John U.S.V.I 00831
(340) 779-2665

GREAT EXUMA, BAHAMAS

Café De Paris
Sandals Emerald Bay
Queens Highway
Great Exuma Bahamas
(888) 726-3257

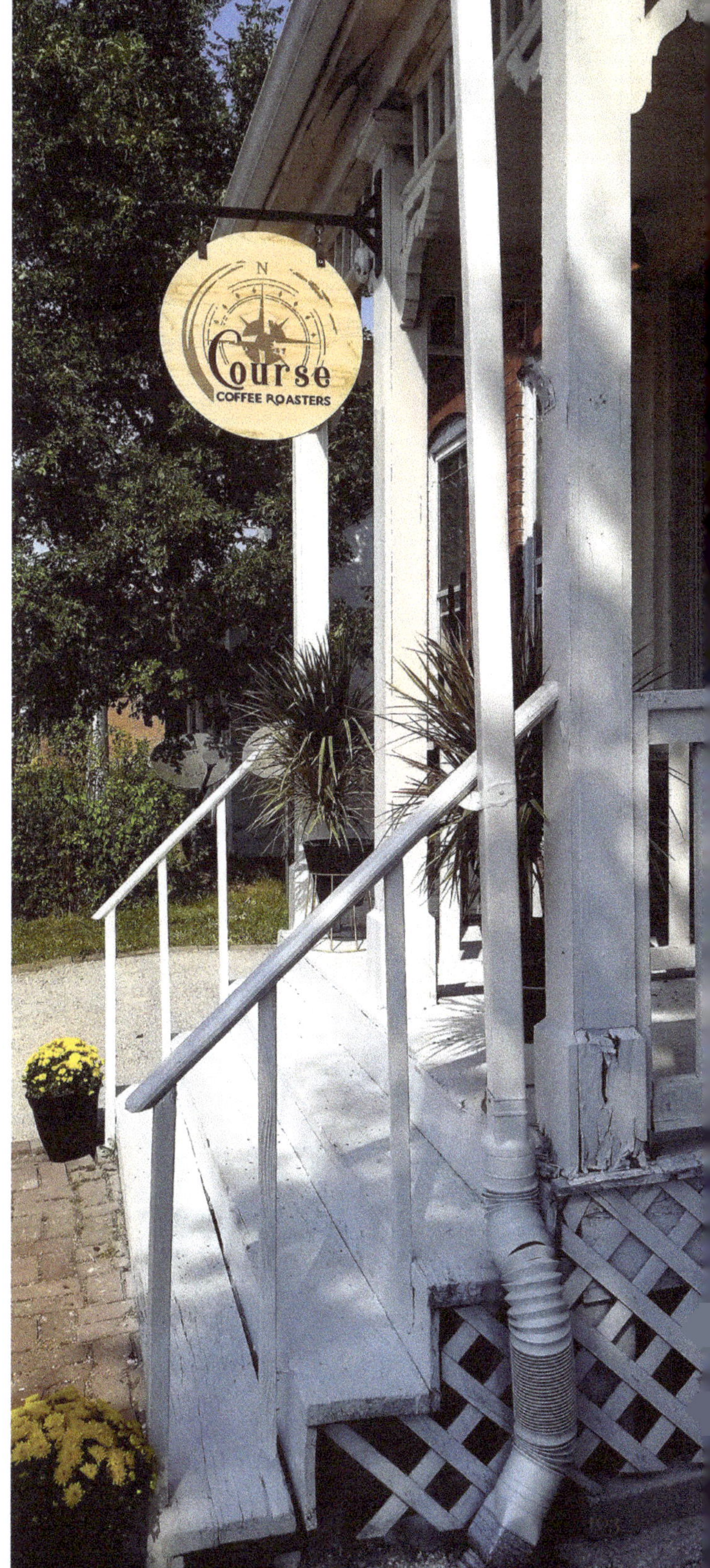

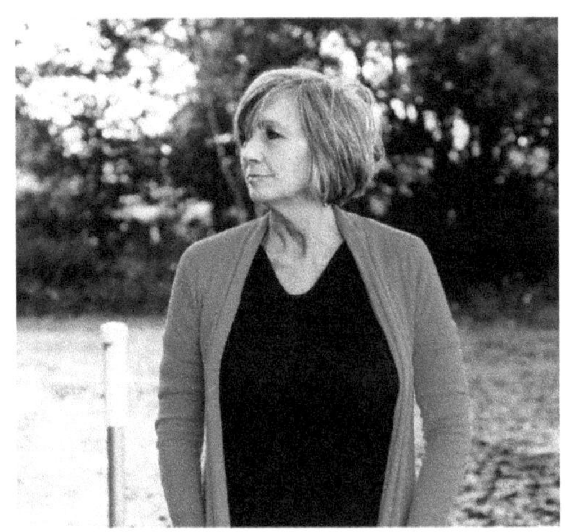

Jessica Lauren Photography

Sheree K. Nielsen believes that every picture tells a story, combining her love of photography and writing with colorful visual descriptions and healing messages found in her poetry, coffee table books, essay collections, and children's books. She finds inspiration in travel, nature, pets, and food . . . especially coffee! As a survivor of Waldenstrom's macroglobulinemia lymphoma, she believes in cherishing every minute of life.

Sheree is author/photographer/poet of 2019 Royal Dragonfly Book Award Winner *Mondays in October* (love songs for the beach), having received First Place in Poetry, Fine Art and Photography and Honorable Mention for Coffee Table Books. She is also the 2015 Da Vinci Eye Award Winner for *Folly Beach Dances* (inspired by the sea and her lymphoma journey), the Chanticleer Little Peeps First Place Category Winner and Montaigne Medal Finalist in 2019 for *Midnight the One-Eyed Cat* (a picture book with co-author Pat Wahler), and the Chanticleer 2019 Finalist for *Ocean Rhythms Kindred Spirits—An Emerson-Inspired Essay Collection on Travel, Nature, Family and Pets.* Her other works are well represented in many travel magazines and publications.

When not writing about her love for coffee in *Coffee Coma*, she's discovering new beaches and cafés with her goofy dogs and patient husband. Five content cats complete her family.

Connect with Sheree at shereenielsen.wordpress.com.

Shanti Arts

Nature ▪ Art ▪ Spirit

Please visit us online
to browse our entire book catalog,
including poetry collections and fiction,
books on travel, nature, healing, art,
photography, and more.

Also take a look at our highly
regarded art and literary journal,
Still Point Arts Quarterly, which
may be downloaded for free.

www.shantiarts.com

www.ingramcontent.com/pod-product-compliance
Lightning Source LLC
LaVergne TN
LVHW060620110826
845147LV00019B/1056

* 9 7 8 1 9 5 1 6 5 1 9 6 1 *